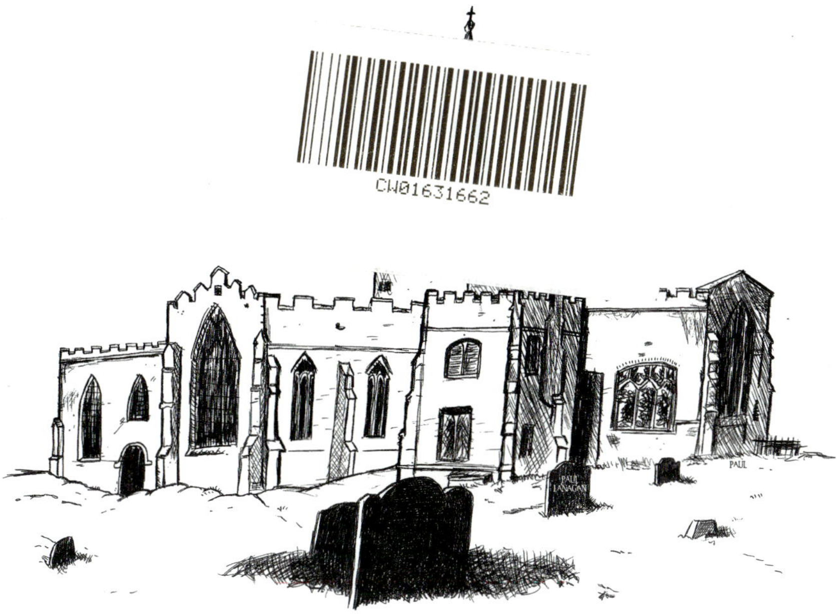

HOUGHTON HERITAGE

HOUGHTON-LE-SPRING
in Old Photographs

VOLUME 1

To William Besoby
Best wishes
Paul Lanagan
18/02/10

by
Paul Lanagan

BOOKS OF THE NORTH

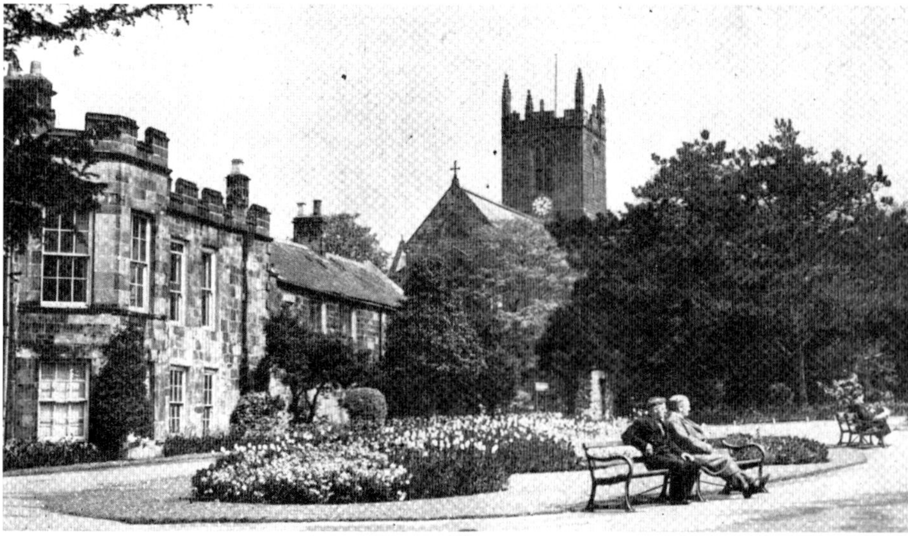

A couple of gents take time out in the newly unveiled Rectory Park, which was taken over as public grounds by Houghton Urban District Council in 1949.

Previous page: A drawing of how St Michael & All Angels Church looked in 1780.

Page 3: Tram No's 20 and 7 stand in the Broadway on the first day of the tramway's operation, Saturday June 10th 1905.

First published in 2010 by Books of the North
ISBN-13: 978-0-9555059-3-5

British Library Cataloguing in Publication Data.
A catalogue record for this book is available from the British Library.

www.houghtonheritage.co.uk

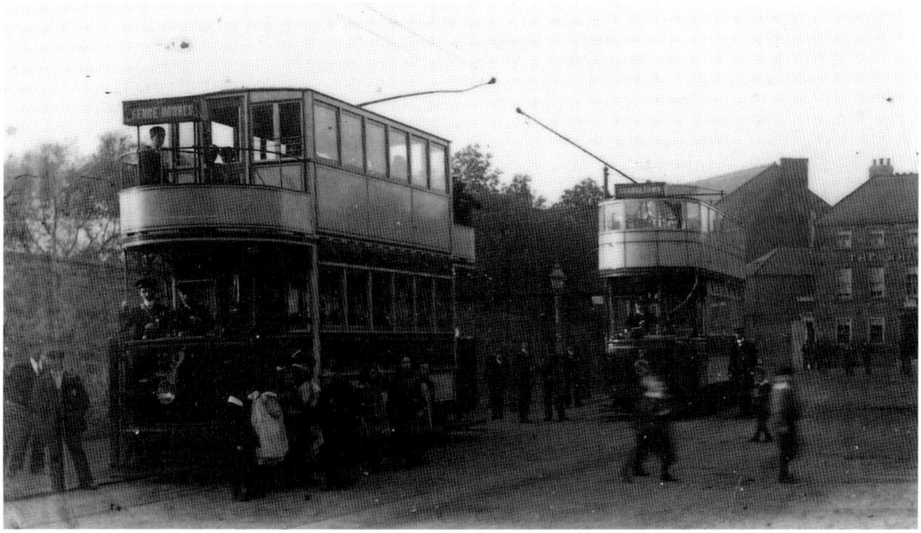

INTRODUCTION

The parish of Houghton-le-Spring is part of the modern City of Sunderland and is located about 6 miles from Durham City in the North East of England. Now a former mining town, Houghton originated as a large rural village though it was undoubtedly a small settlement in the early years, perhaps in the form of a fortified Saxon Burh. Excavations at Copt Hill have revealed that humans inhabited this area during the Mesolithic period, about 7000 years ago.

Houghton-le-Spring takes its name from the Anglo-Saxon 'Hogh' which means a point of land projected into a plain, and the Old English word 'tun' which means settlement. This can translate to: 'homestead or settlement on the spur of a hill', which is rather apt when one approaches the town from the Cut. Recorded simply as 'Hoctona' in the Boldon Book of 1183, the addition of Le Spring has several possible origins. Some suggest it is derived from the Le Spring family, Lords of Houghton in ancient times, such as Sir John le Spring who was killed in his own manor house in 1313 by Robert Lascelles, his lover's husband! Another explanation, which is backed up by a 'Regester Booke belonginge to the Paryshe of Houghton in the Springe' from 1598, is based around the medicinal springs which flow from the surrounding magnesian limestone rocks, while Churchwarden records for the ancient St Michael & All Angels Church list the name as 'Houghton in le Spring' in 1638.

As an historian, my main concern is with corroborating tangible facts relating to the social history of our town, and as such my interests tend to focus on the Victorian period through to recent times. Indeed, many of the photographs in this book reflect this. They have been ordered in such a way that they will take you on a journey along Houghton's well known streets, with a chance to see many faces along the way. Most have not been shared before and will be new to the reader while some are old favourites but have been presented in a new light owing to the advances in digital printing technology.

Paul Lanagan

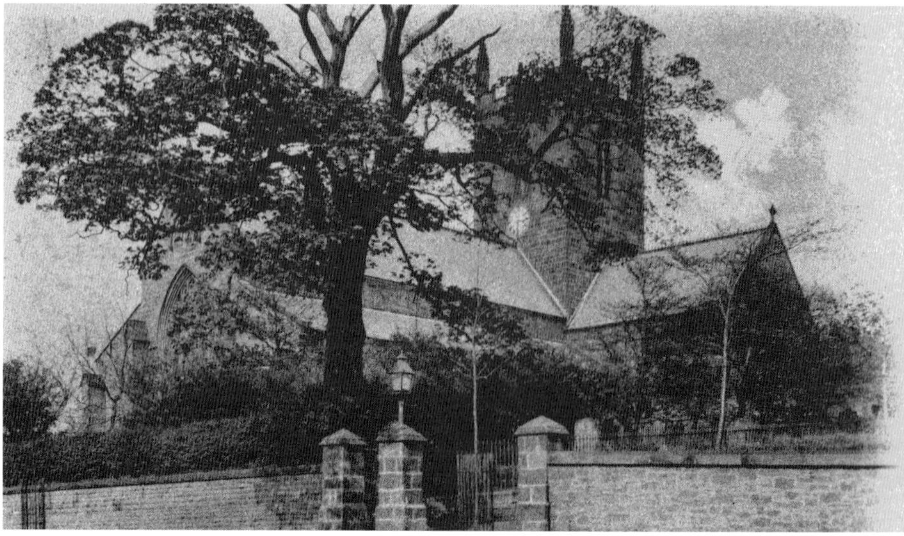

The historic St Michael & All Angels Parish Church at the turn of the twentieth century, with the original entrance to the churchyard. The excavations of 2008 suggest that parts of the church date from the Saxon period, while there may have been an earlier Roman building on the site.

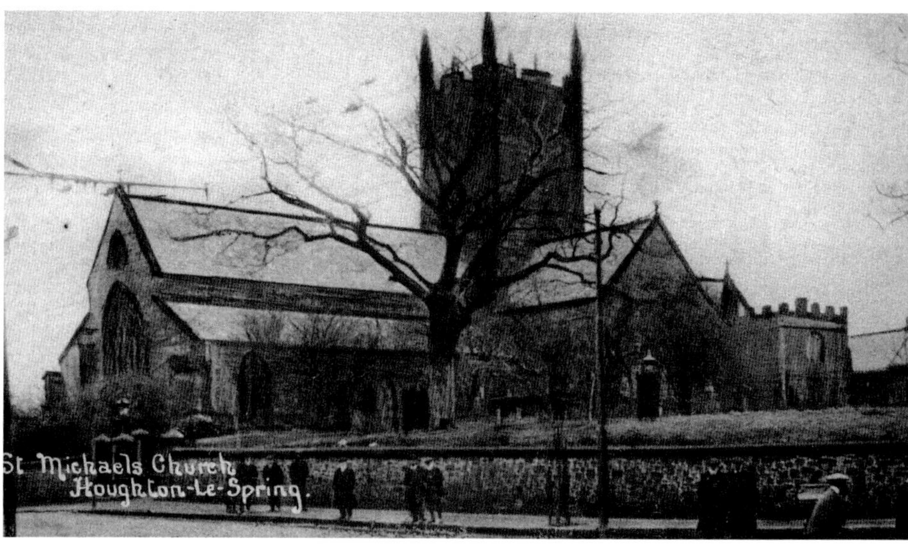

Looking across Durham Road to St Michael's Church on a cold winter day in the early 1920s. The Church's appearance has changed dramatically over the years: the tower dates from 1824 and replaced an octagonal wooden spire (see page 1), while the high pitched roof was added during restoration work by the well-known Newcastle architect, John Dobson, in 1857.

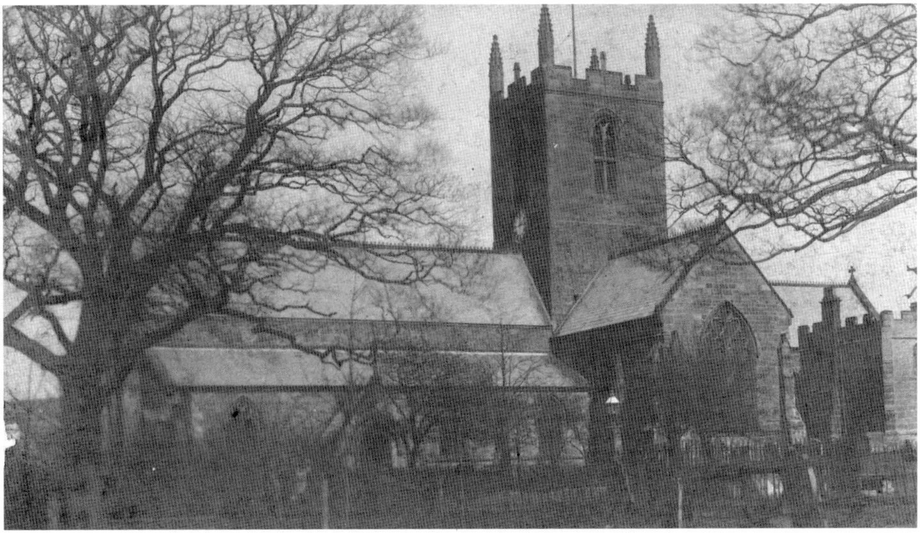

A rare early photograph of St Michael's Church surrounded by headstones, circa 1900. More than 8500 interments took place in the churchyard between 1793 and its closure on August 11th 1854, when it became full following a cholera epidemic.

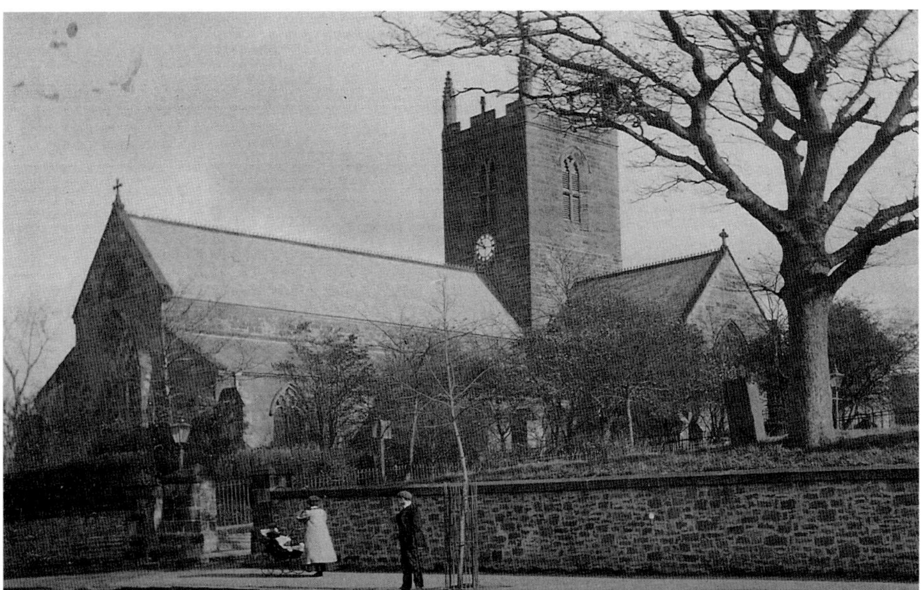

A lady pushes her perambulator along Durham Road as the church tower looks down, circa 1930. Note the hedgerow which obscured the front view of the church for many years.

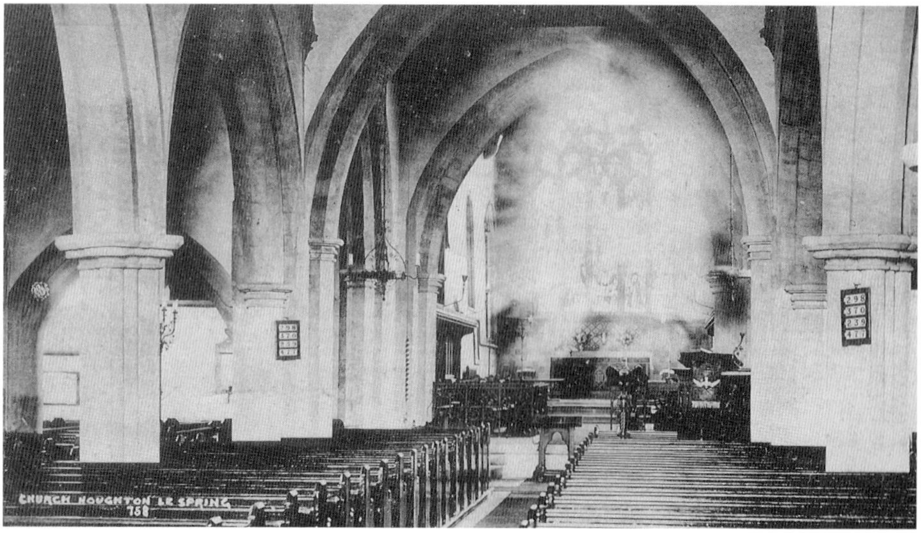

A rare interior view of St Michael's Church, taken circa 1890 when the church was lit by candlelight. The view shows the chancel before the screen was erected in memory of Thomas W. U. Robinson, who died in 1888. The Victorian pews were removed in 2008 when the church interior was reordered.

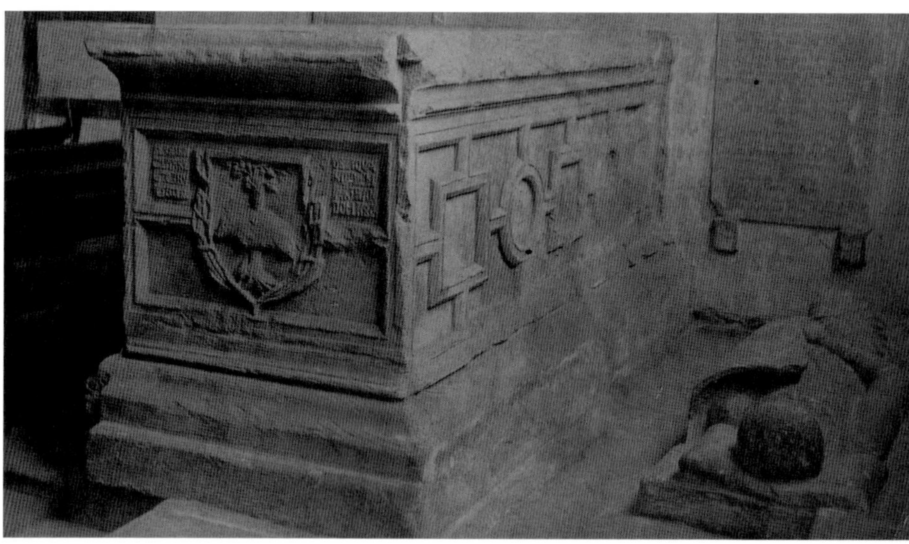

This simple altar tomb was the final resting place of Bernard Gilpin, Rector of Houghton 1558 until 1583, however keyhole camera investigations have revealed the tomb to be empty. The raised inscription on the tomb reads: *BERNERD GILPIN RECTOR HVIVS ECCLIOE – OBIIT QVARTO DIE MARTII AN DOM. 1583*, and translates as: *Bernard Gilpin, Rector of this Church, died on the 4th day of March in the year of our Lord 1583.*

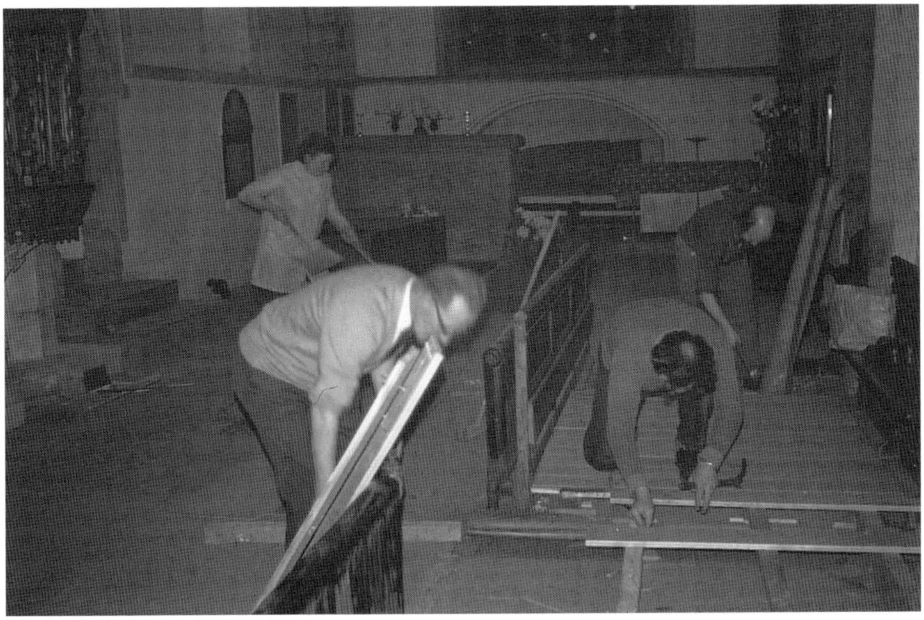

Looking towards the south transept of St Michael's while parishioners make preparations for the new altar platform, circa 1972. Building the platform are, from left: Marjorie Bartlett, Church Stewardess; Fred Bartlett, Church Treasurer; Brian Rutherford; and Ron Knowles.

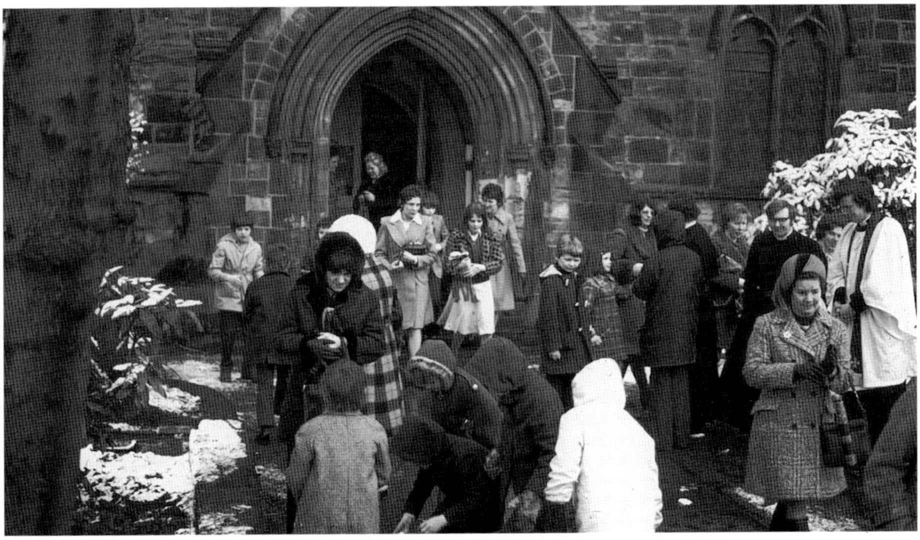

Parishioners leaving St Michael's Church after the 9:30am service in the 1970s. The church doorway is very similar in shape to the stone lych gate at the churchyard's detached extension on Sunderland Street. The worn threshold stone of the south doorway of the early Norman church was discovered during the 2008 excavations inside the Church.

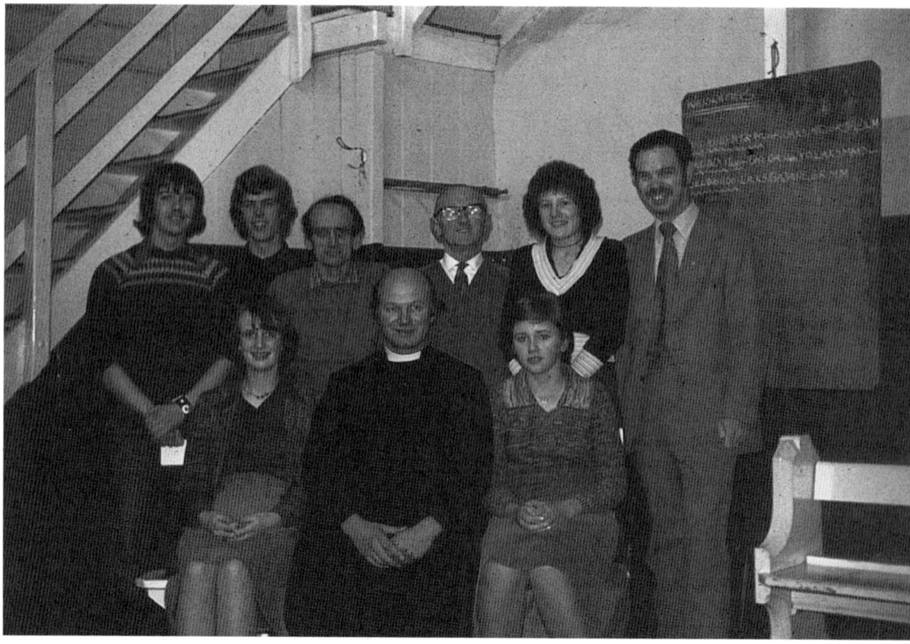

Rector Peter Brett, centre, poses with the bell ringers in St Michael's belfry in the 1970s. A full peal of eight bells had been installed in the tower in 1928.

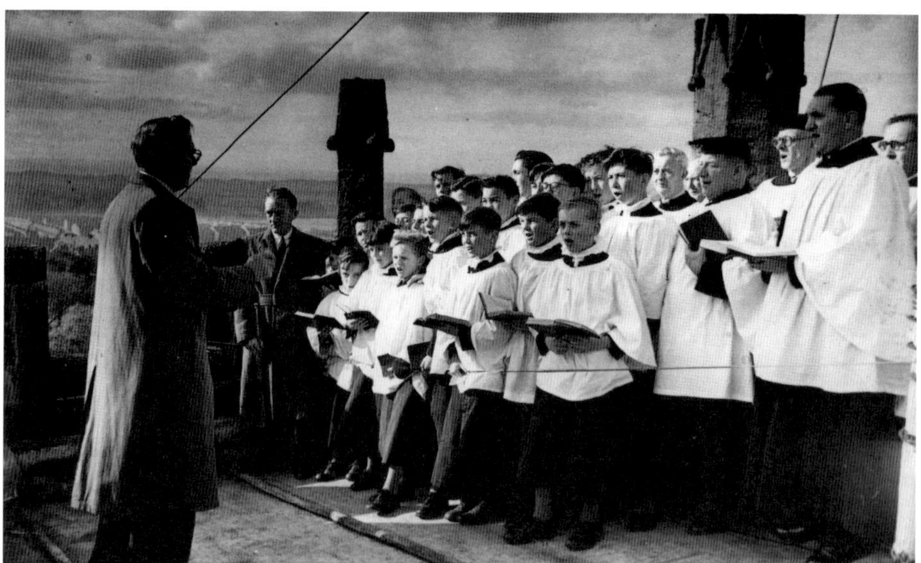

The choir sings from the top of St Michael's Church during Houghton Feast in the 1950s, as was the tradition for many years. It was normal for visitors to ascend the tower for a small fee during the church's summer fair in years gone by.

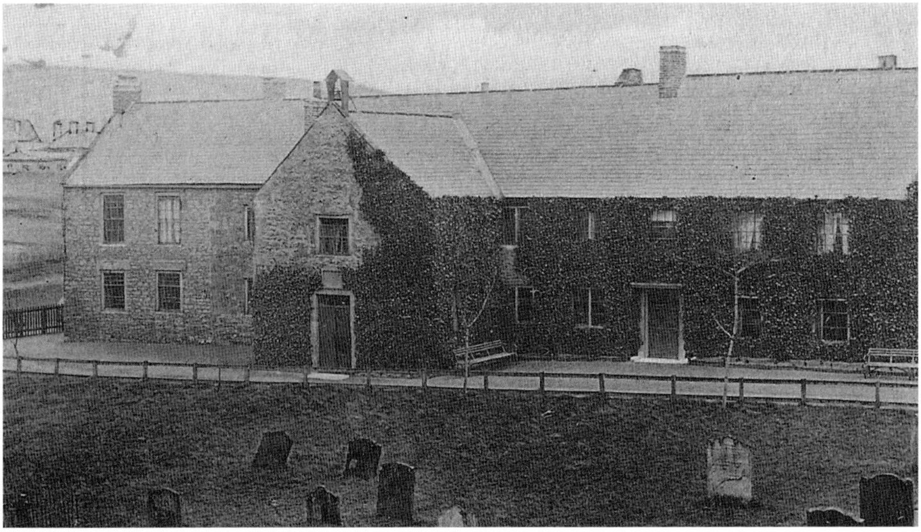

The Royal Kepier Grammar School, as seen here around 1900, received its Royal Charter on April 2nd 1574, signed by Elizabeth I. The school was founded by Houghton Rector, Bernard Gilpin, and his friend John Heath, a London merchant who owned the Hospital of St Giles of Kepier, next to Gilesgate, Durham. The school, which closed in 1922, had many distinguished alumni during its 350 year history, including Sir Lindsay Wood, Christopher Cookson, and Thomas Elliot Harrison.

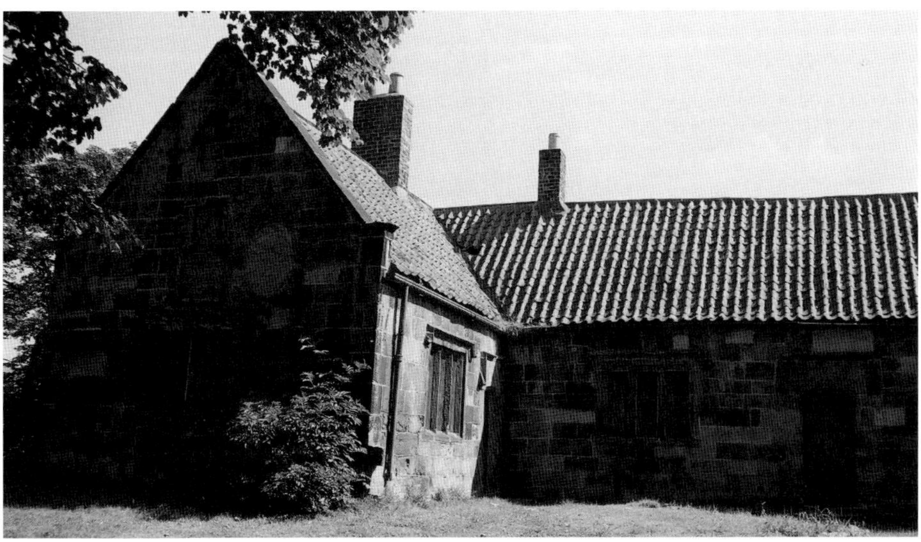

The Davenport and Lilburne Almshouses in 1973, five years before they were modernised. The buildings, which are located next to the Kepier School in the churchyard, feature two dedication stones which read as follows: *'George Lilburne Esq. built the moiety of this hospital at his own charge, and endowed it with ten pounds per annum forever for the maintenance of three poor people. Anno Dom. 1668.'* and *'The charitable intention of the Reverend William Sharp M.A., carried into effect by Miss Dorothy Spearman his heiress by will, added to the Revenues of the Almshouse £18 per annum.'*

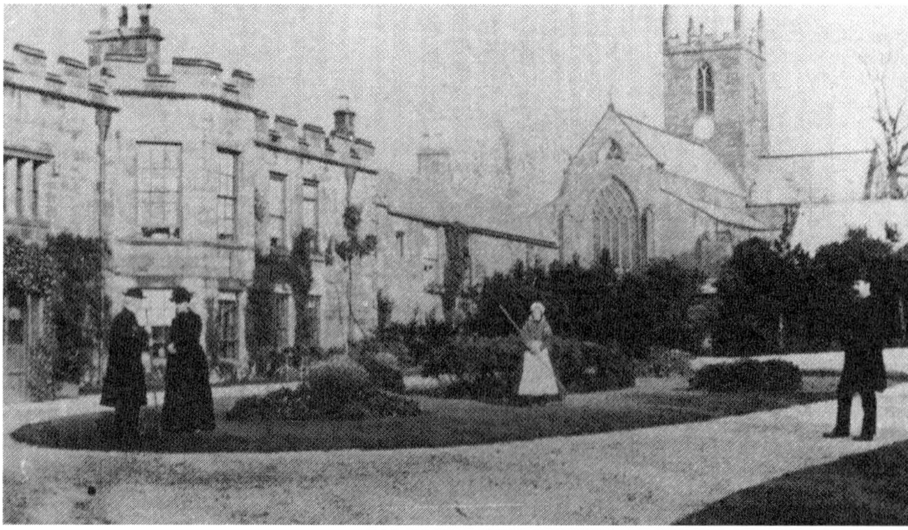

A rare photo from around 1890 of Rector John Grey and his wife outside the Rectory. Their lady gardener, Alice Hamilton, can be seen tending to the flower beds, centre, as an unknown gentleman watches. The old Rector, who had come to Houghton in 1847, died on November 11th 1895 and was interred in his controversial Hillside Cemetery.

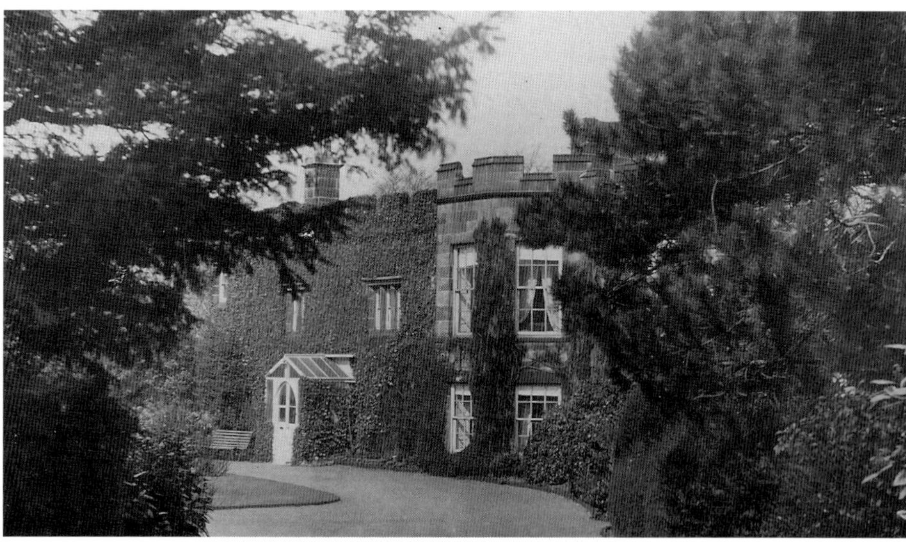

A view of Houghton Rectory, as ivy creeps around the building, in the 1920s. Successive photos from the early 1900s show that the ivy enveloped the building at an astonishing rate, almost covering the front by 1945.

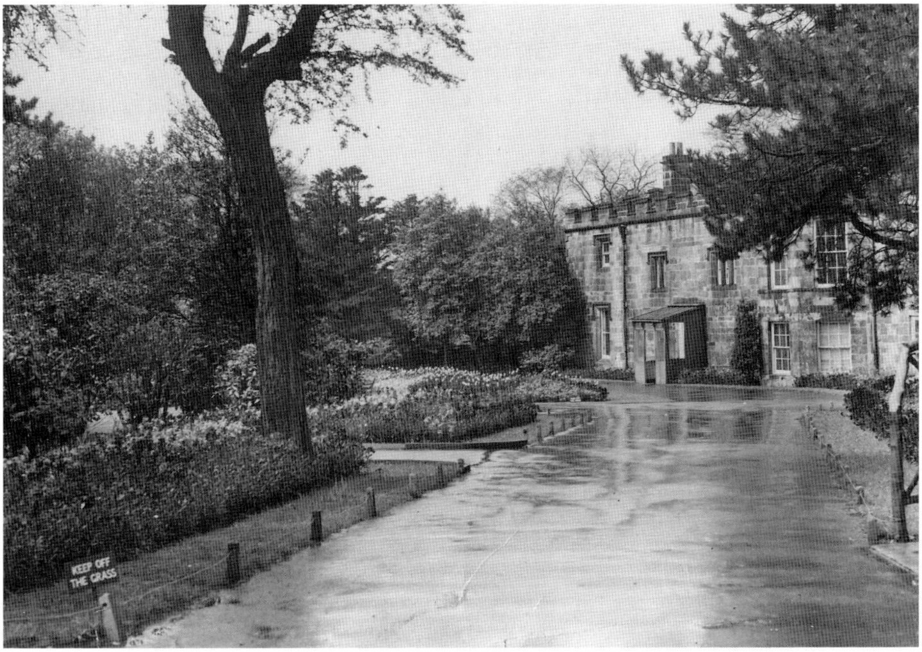

The Rectory and grounds shortly after they were turned over as a public park in 1949. The ivy was pruned and large parts of the building were demolished. Note the sign, left, 'Keep Off The Grass'. The Park Keeper at this time was Charles Barratt, who was popular with the children during conker time.

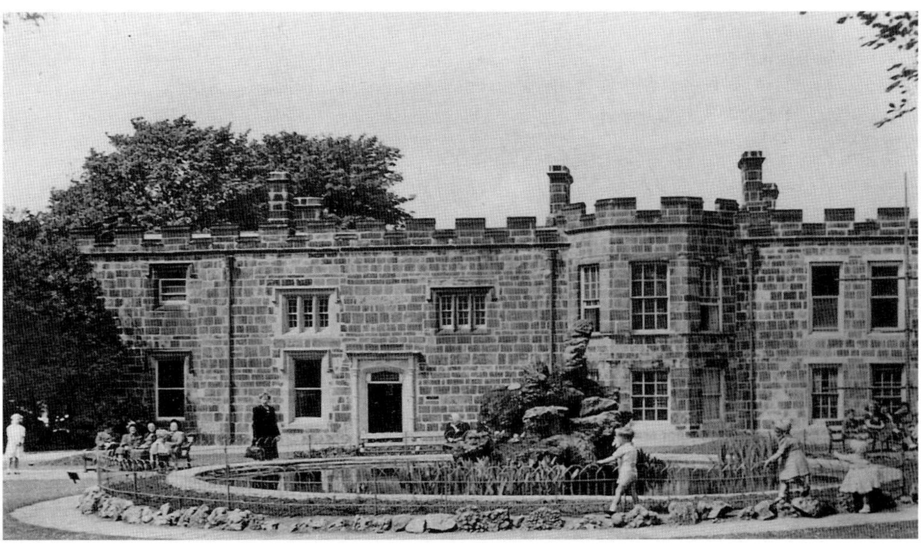

Children play around one of the impressive fountains to have graced the Rectory gardens over the years, as seen here in the 1950s. Does any reader know when the present fountain dates from?

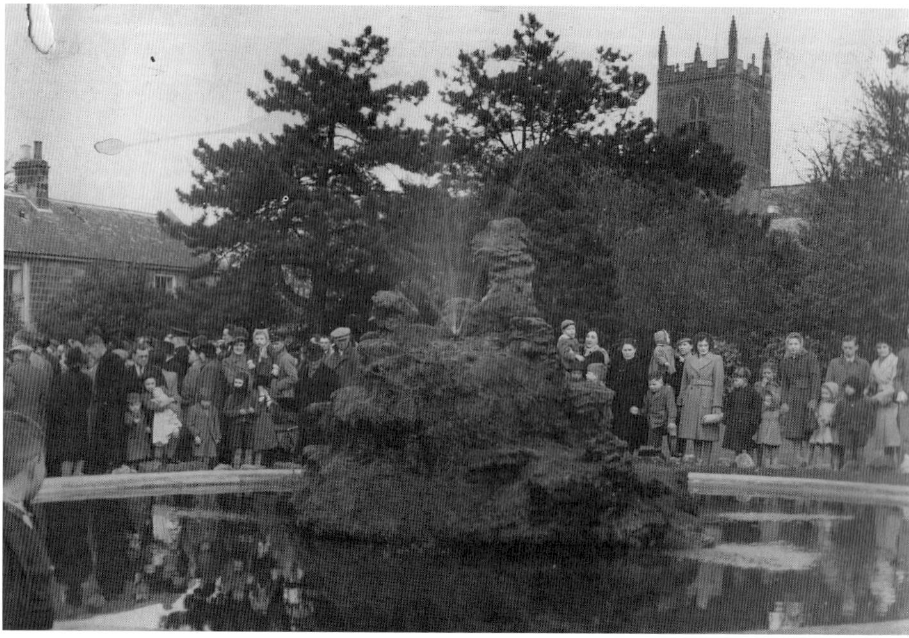

Houghtonians gather round the Rectory fountain when the grounds were unveiled as a public park in 1949. It is thought that the Park opened in June but many of the people are wearing winter clothing.

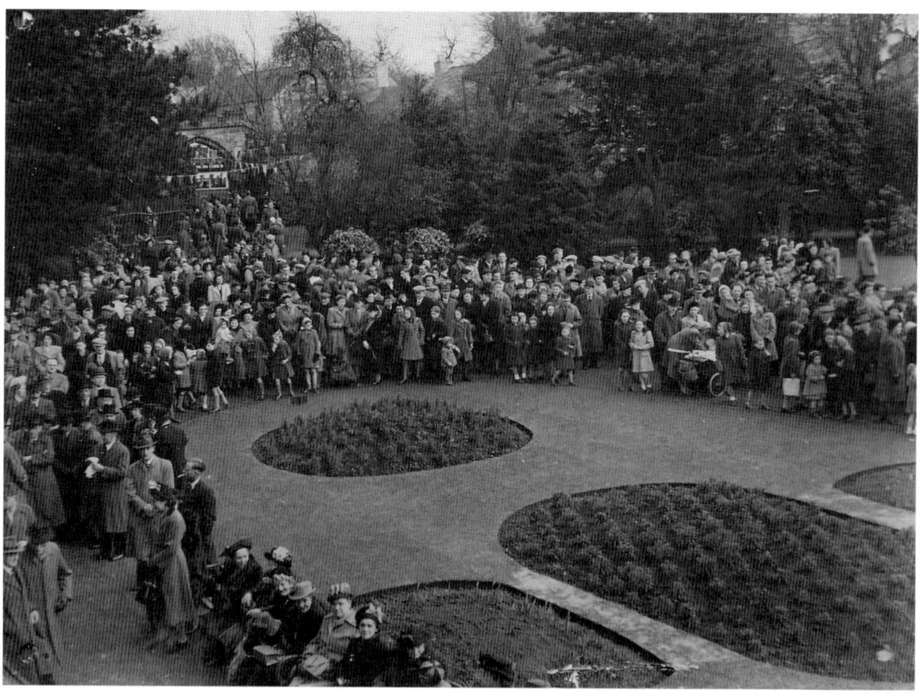

This view, taken from the upper floor of the Rectory, shows the huge crowds attending the Park's official opening. The children at the front are struggling to obey the signs and keep off the grass!

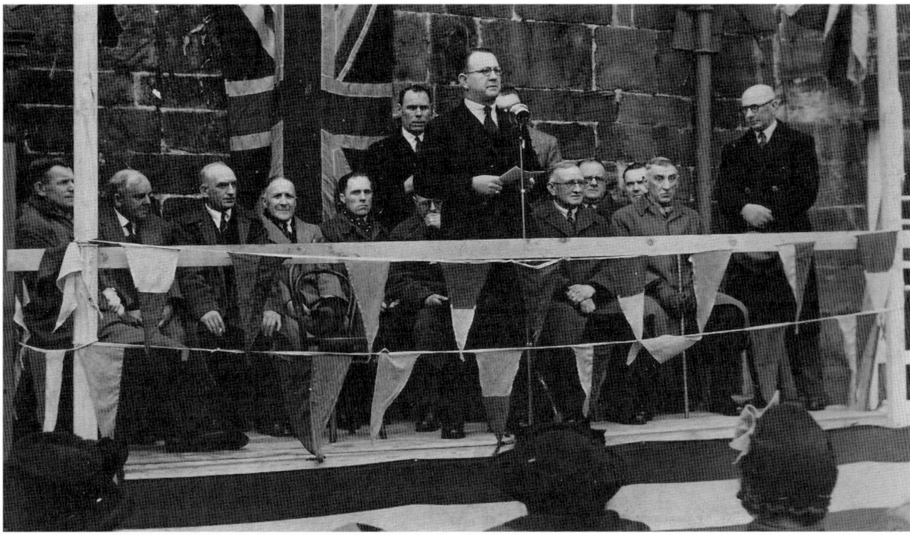

Union flags adorn the Rectory building while officials from Houghton Urban District Council make speeches at the Rectory Park's official opening day in 1949. Pictured are: Councillor Jim Lowery (third from left); W. H. Dinsley, Chairman of the Council (at the microphone); and W. W. Plews, Clerk to the Council (far right). The speeches that day touched upon the history of Houghton and led to the publication of a book on the town's history by Frank H. Rushford in 1950.

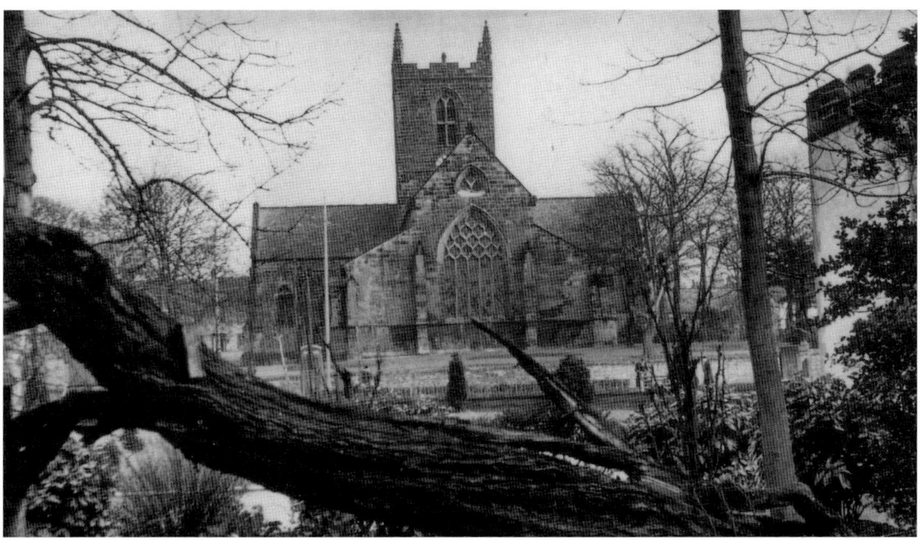

The ancient Gilpin Thorn as seen growing in the grounds of the Rectory Park, circa 1950. This hawthorn is thought to have grown from a cutting taken from the legendary Glastonbury Thorn by Bernard Gilpin in the late 1500s but sadly died at the hands of vandals in the 1990s.

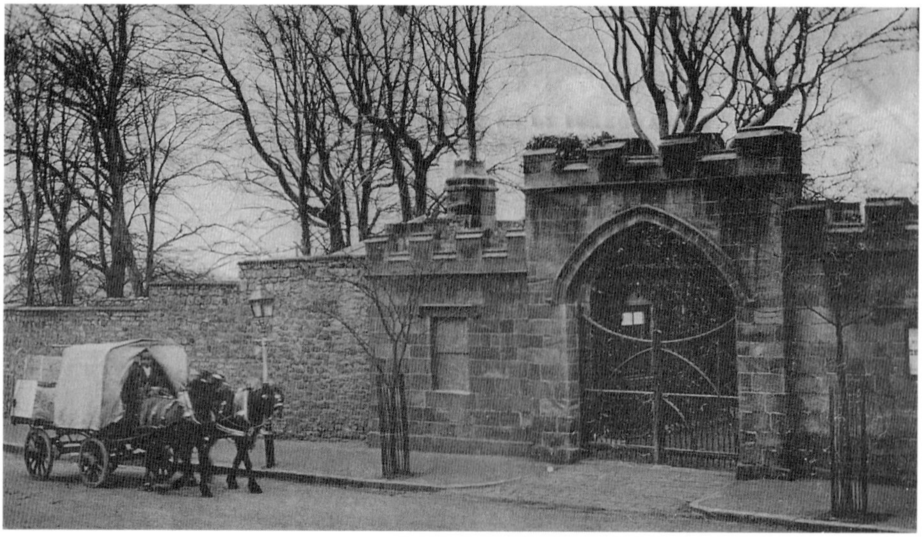

Horses and cart trundle along past the Rectory archway and gatehouse, circa 1900. To the right of the archway was St Michael's Church Hall, which was formally opened by the Bishop of Durham on January 10th 1882.

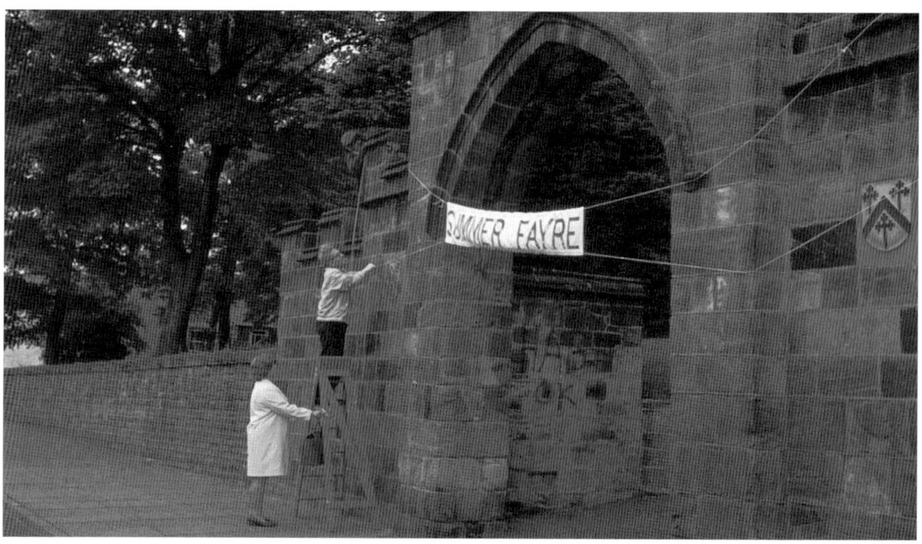

Sheila Mackie holds the ladder as Sid Macey helps to erect a banner for the Church's summer fayre, circa 1977. Fred Bartlett, the Church Treasurer, can be seen at the top of the battlement. The archway was relocated from the other side of the road when the Urban District Council took over the Rectory and grounds. Four shields were incorporated into the archway in 1953 and pay homage to the See of Durham and three of Houghton's Rectors: William Sancroft, Bernard Gilpin and George Davenport.

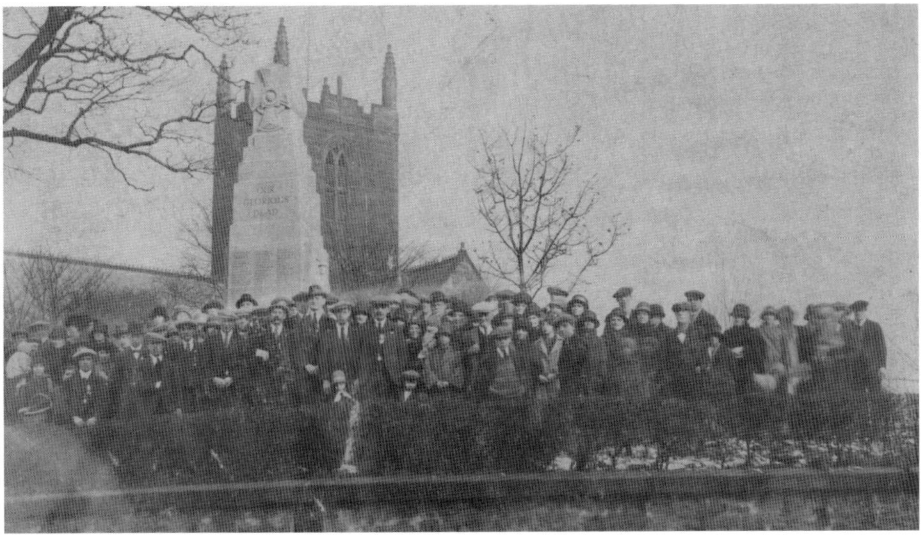

Houghton folk turn out for the unveiling of the new cenotaph on November 7th 1925. The memorial, which is located in the southwest corner of the churchyard, was made from Portland stone at a cost of £7,000 and features the names of 236 individuals who were killed during the Great War of 1914 - 1918.

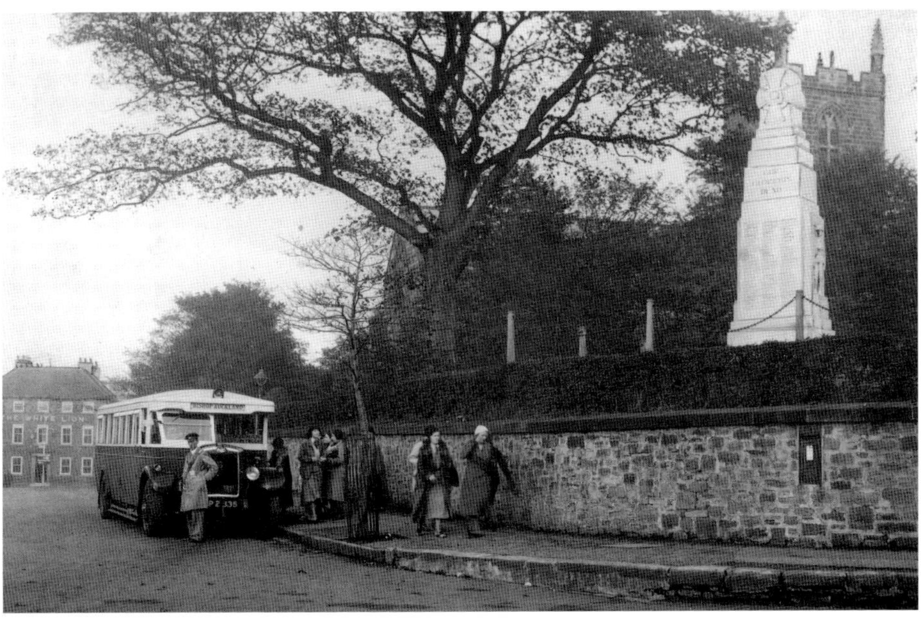

Female passengers disembark from a bus below the cenotaph in 1932. The bus is destined for Bishop Auckland via Durham and Spennymoor.

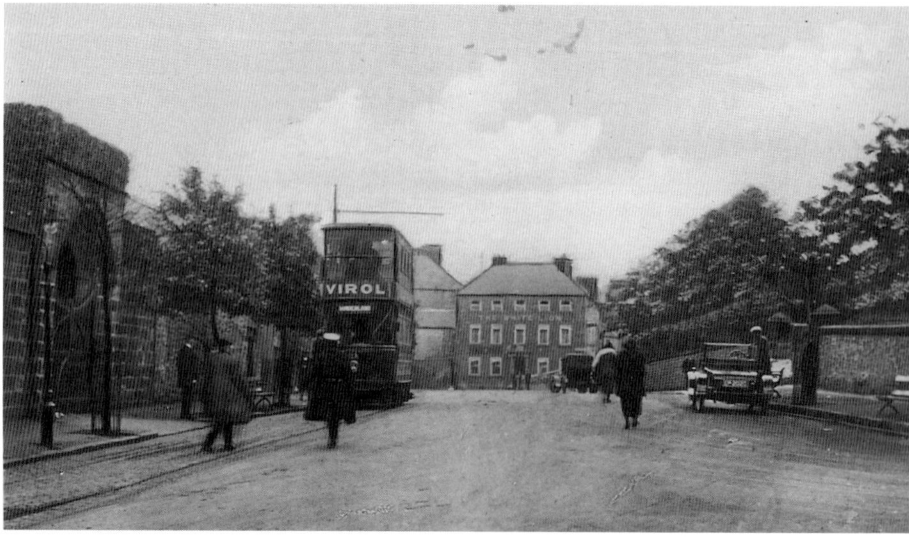

Tram number 21 of the Sunderland District Electric Tramways fleet stops at the terminus outside the Rectory grounds around 1920. The product being advertised on this particular tram is Virol, a malt based vitamin preparation.

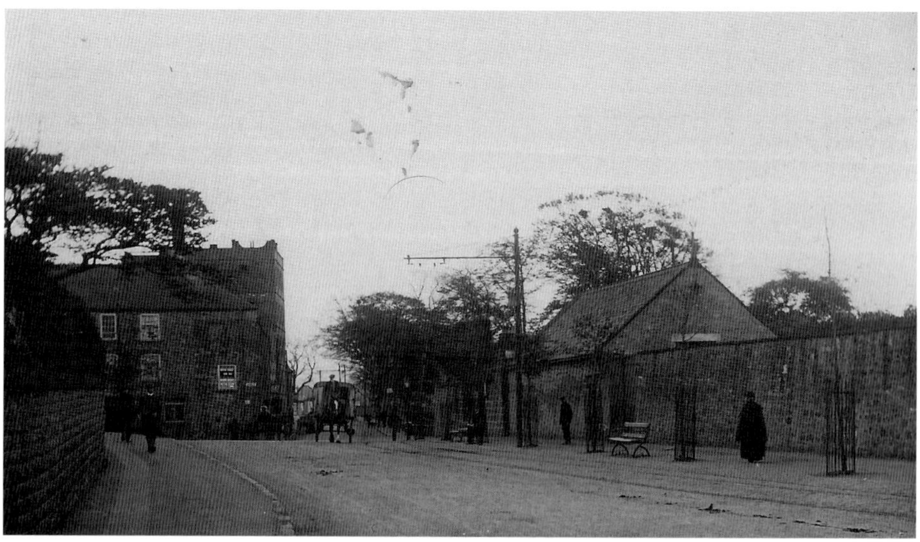

A rare southerly view of Durham Road, revealing the other side of St Michael's Hall, circa 1910. The Red Lion Inn can be seen on the corner of Church Street, left, while the then five storey King's Hall can be seen in the background. In later years a policeman stood on point duty on these crossroads.

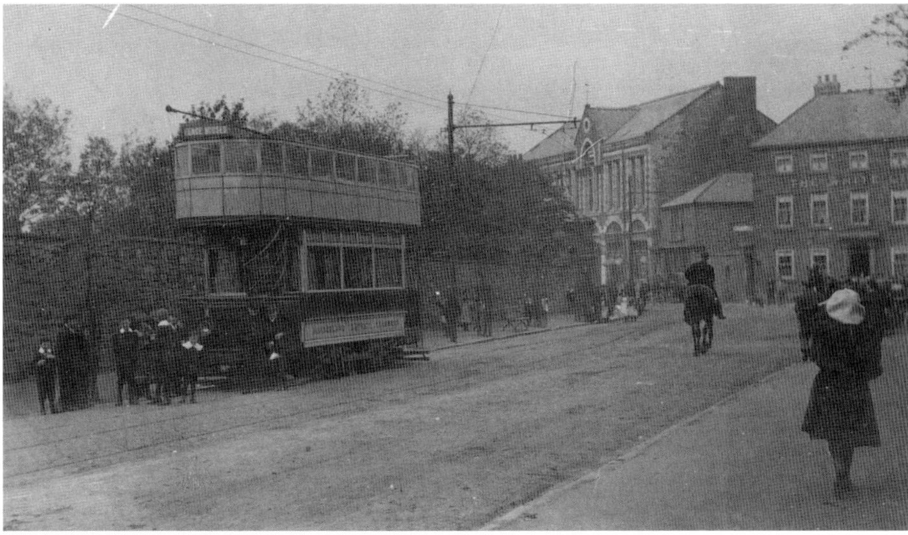

Houghton's tram network often provided rare opportunities for the public to be photographed, as this view from around 1910 shows. The trams were in operation for a relatively short period of time, 1905 until 1925, and were eventually replaced by buses.

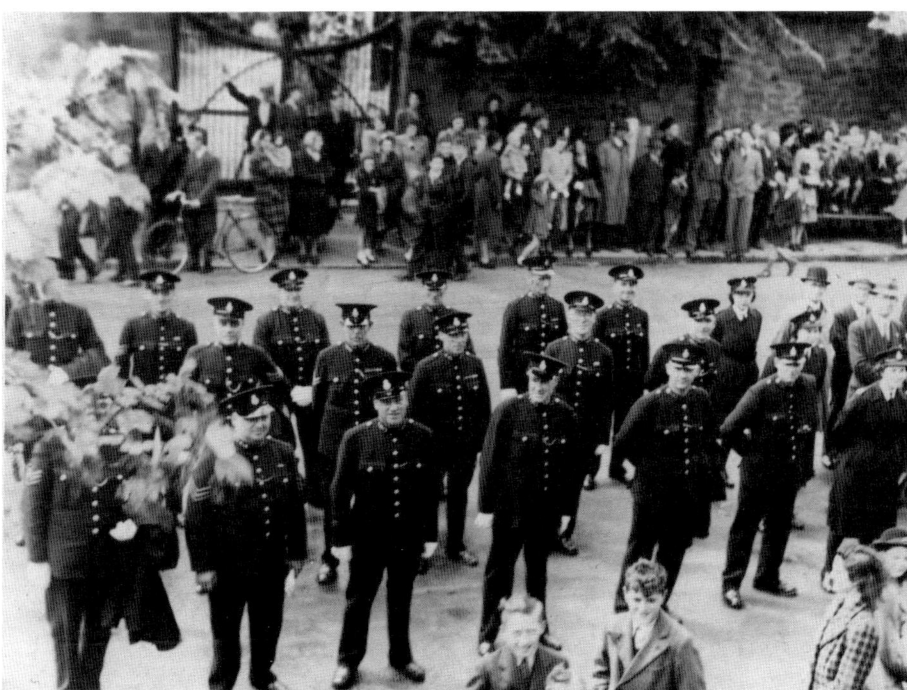

Members of the public gather along Durham Road in front of St Michael's Church to watch a parade in 1942. The Rectory gates can be seen in the background.

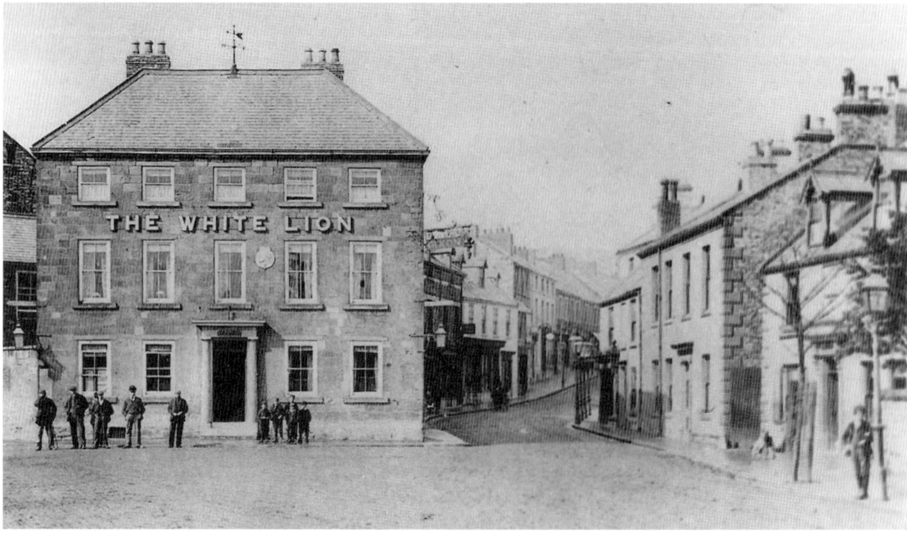

The White Lion public house standing at the fork in the road between Newbottle Street, left, and Sunderland Street, right, around 1895. This building was demolished during the redevelopment of Houghton for the A690 dual-carriageway in the 1960s and was replaced with a less impressive building. The Golden Lion pub, seen on the right, survived the mania and is still there to this day.

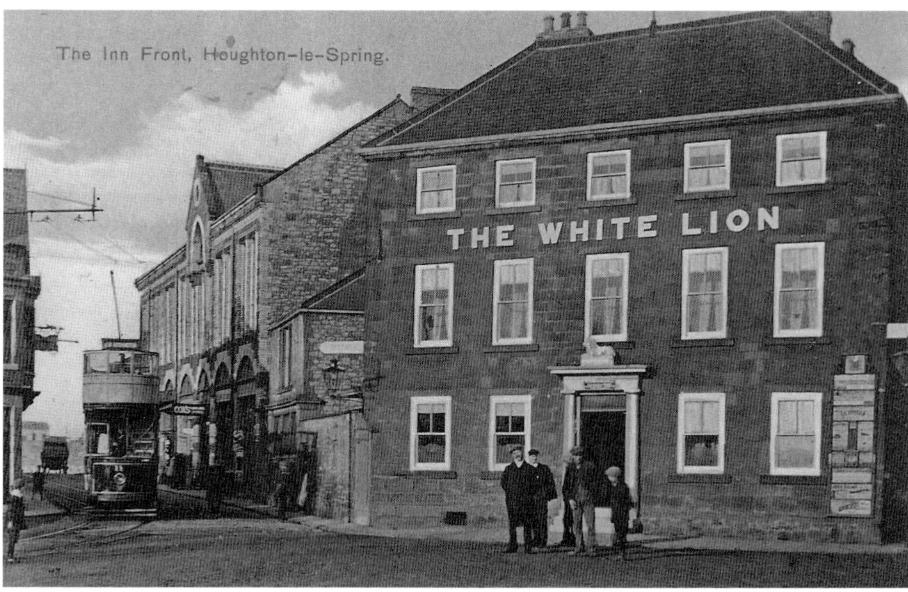

Regulars from the White Lion gather outside to be photographed as a tram trundles along Newbottle Street, circa 1920. The Houghton Tramways route ran from Grangetown to Ryhope, Tunstall to Silksworth, East Herrington to Herrington Burn, Philadelphia, Newbottle and on to Houghton. Branches extended to Penshaw railway station via Shiney Row from Herrington Burn, and to Fencehouses station via Colliery Row and Dubmire. In 1906 the route, which covered 14.28 miles, was extended south to Hetton-le-Hole and Easington Lane.

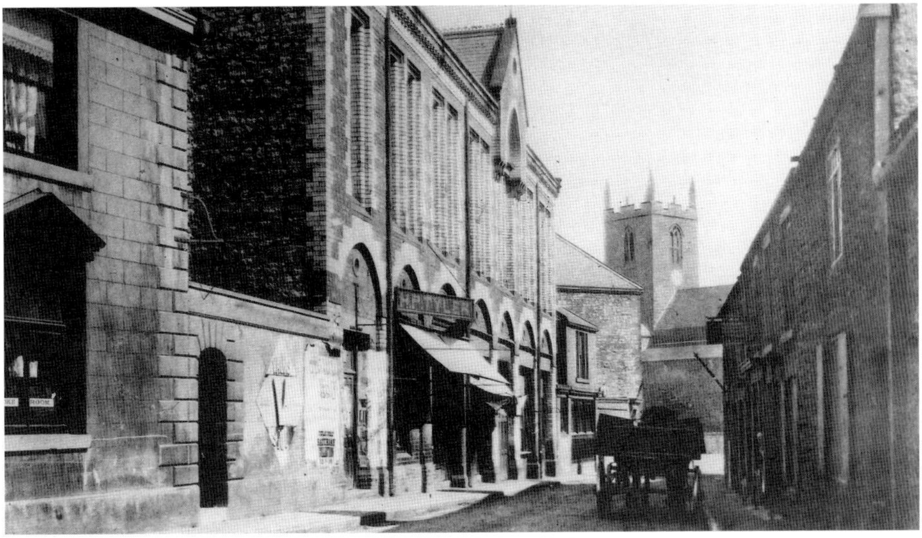

Newbottle Street, looking towards St Michael's Church with the Town Hall on the left, around 1895. The Town Hall was inaugurated on December 30th 1873 and had an upper floor which measured 75ft by 24ft, while the lower floor housed an indoor market with seventeen shops inside and several facing out onto Newbottle Street. In the early years, the building was known as the Town Hall Picture Palace and had a capacity of 800 with 250 in the circle.

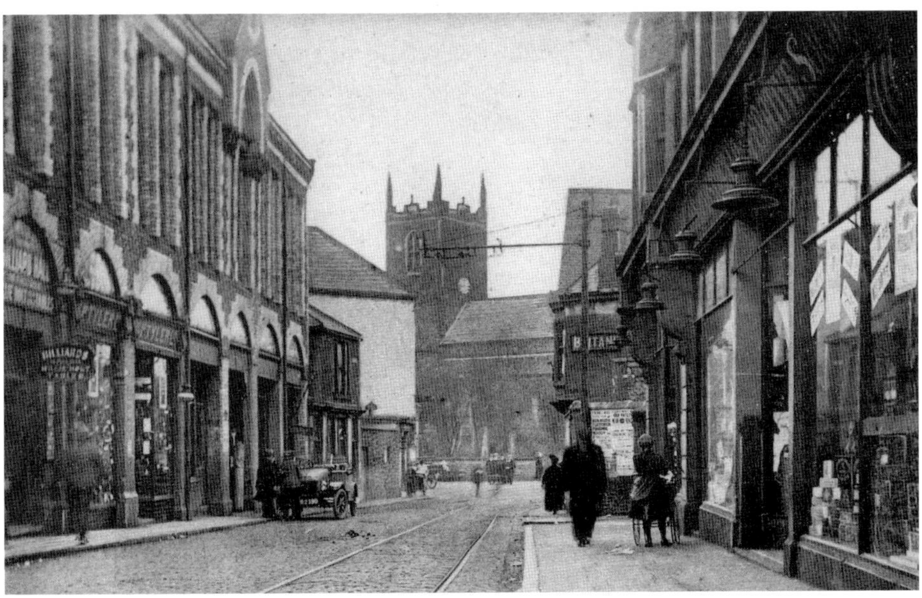

A similar view of the Town Hall on Newbottle Street, around 1920. By this time the upper floor had been converted into a billiards hall with fourteen Willie Holt tables on two floors, while the properties on the right side of the street had been developed into a branch of the Newbottle & District Co-operative Society (see also page 21).

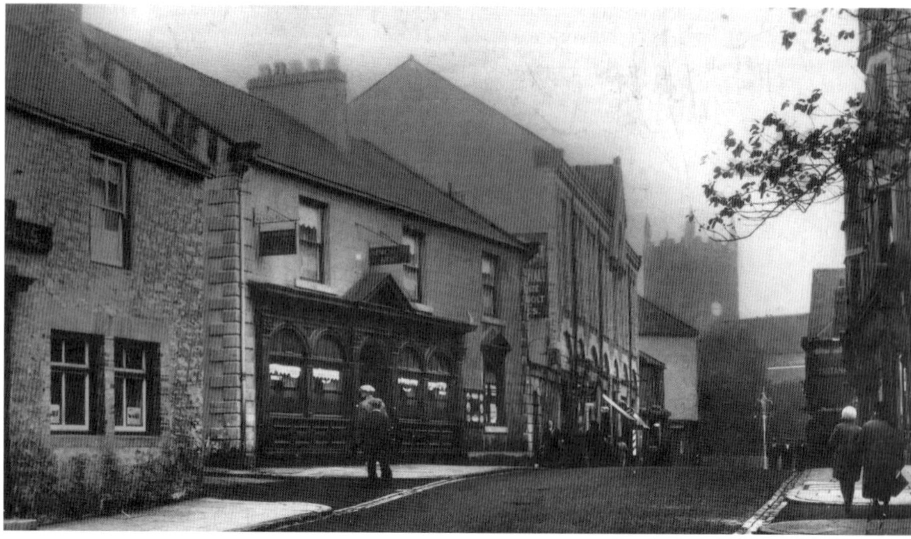

A couple of gents on Newbottle Street look up the access road to Pottery Yard, circa 1930. This small road was sandwiched between two public houses, the Royal Oak Inn on the left, and the Newcastle Arms on the right.

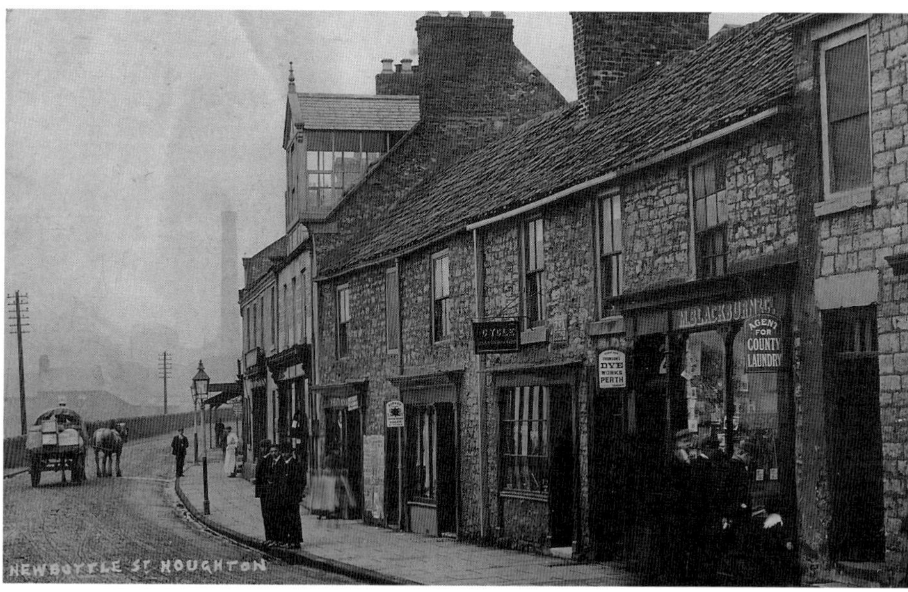

A view of the east side of Newbottle Street, circa 1900, some seven years before the west side of the street was constructed. The prominent shop in the foreground, 23 Newbottle Street, is occupied by M. Blackburn & Co, newsagents, with John G. Shearer, cycle agent, next door.

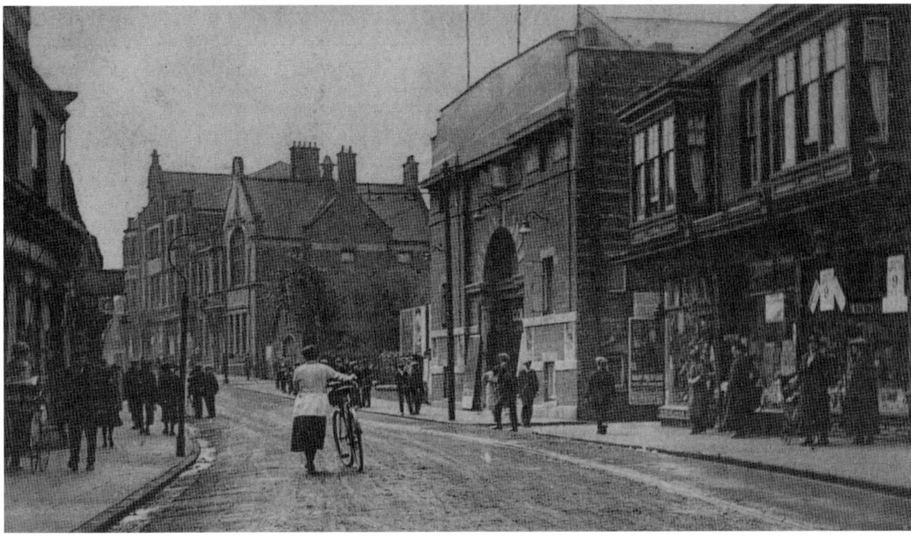

John Lishman and Norman Robinson's Coliseum Cinema, centre, dominates Newbottle Street with its arched doorway, circa 1924. The premises opened in the summer of 1921 and were in use until its closure on January 24th 1960, when it was converted into a supermarket. The building is currently occupied by a health and beauty retailer.

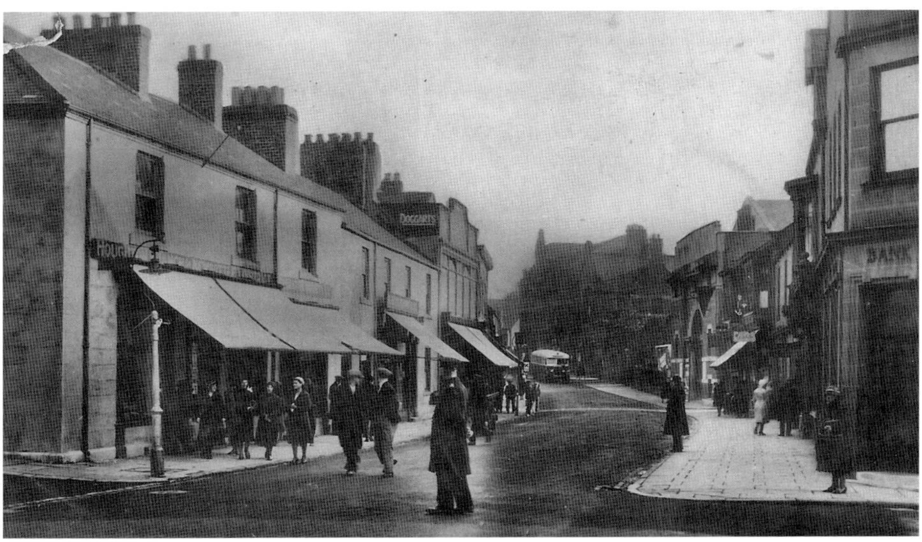

The centre of Newbottle Street in the 1940s. The Houghton branch of the Newbottle & District Co-operative Society can be seen on the left. Opposite, on the right, is a branch of Barclays Bank which opened in 1922.

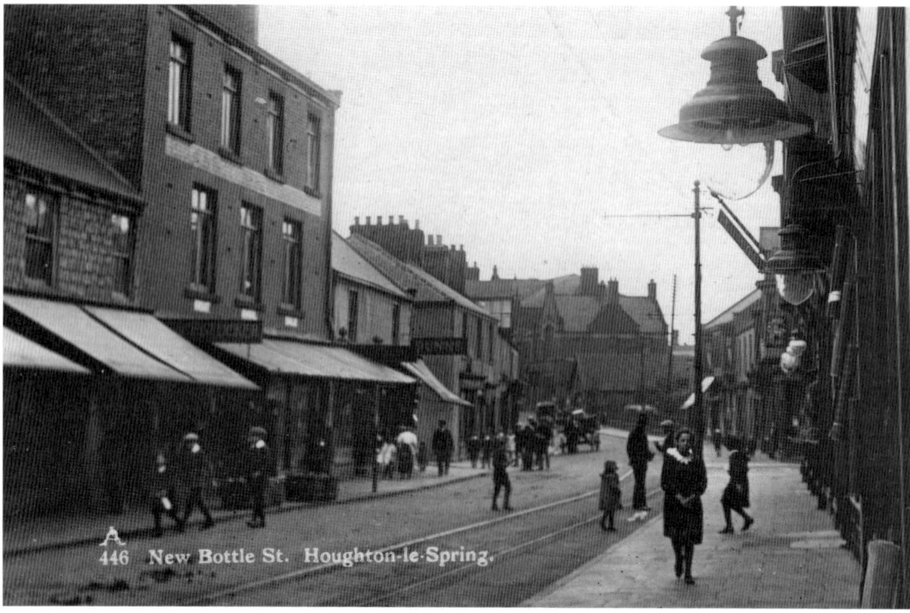

Looking along Newbottle Street around 1915, with tramlines clearly visible in the road. The business sign of Bruce & Tucker, drapers, can be seen on the left. This firm was located at 43 - 45 Newbottle Street and in 1954 became known as Booth & Bruce.

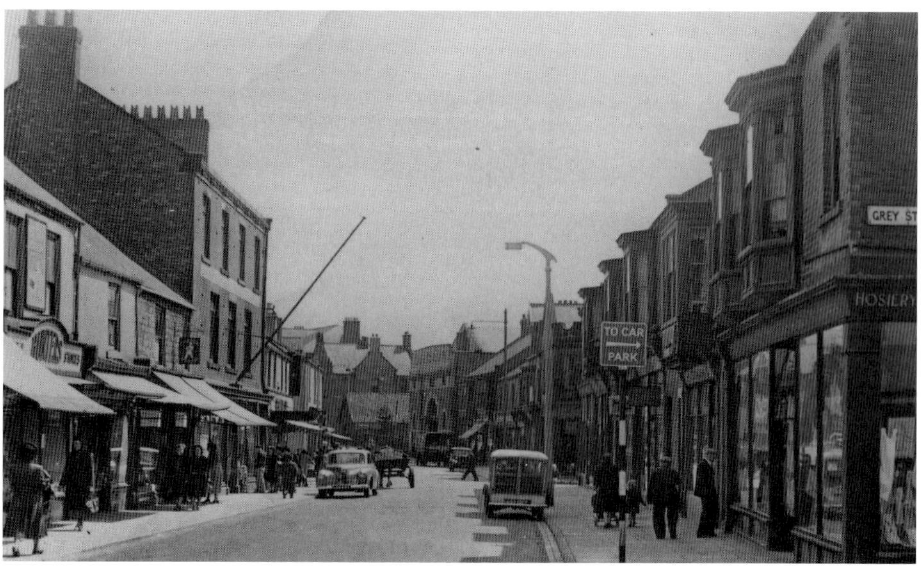

A similar view of Newbottle Street, this time in the 1950s. The premises of the Johnston Brothers, drapery and hosiery makers, can be seen on the corner of Grey Street, right.

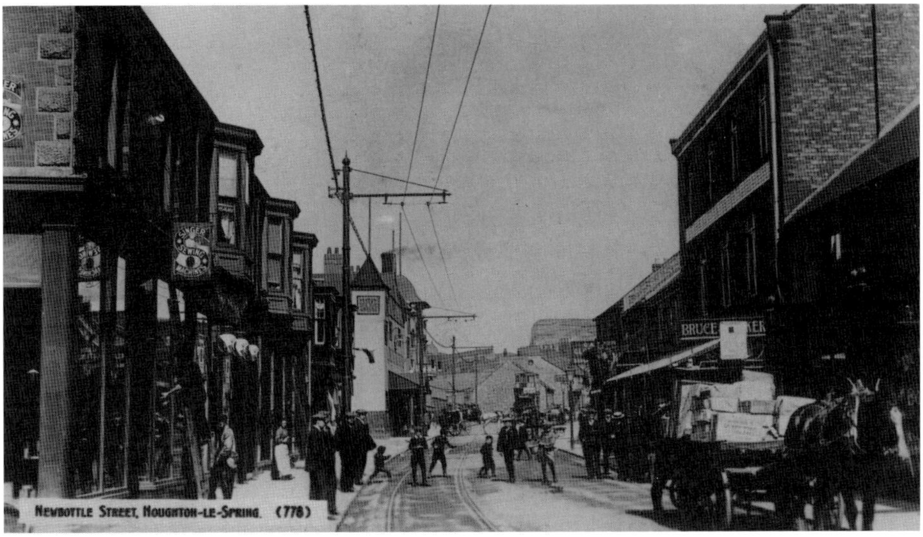

A busy scene at the north section of Newbottle Street, around 1916, with children playing on the tracks as a tram approaches from the distance. An amusement arcade now occupies the property on the left corner.

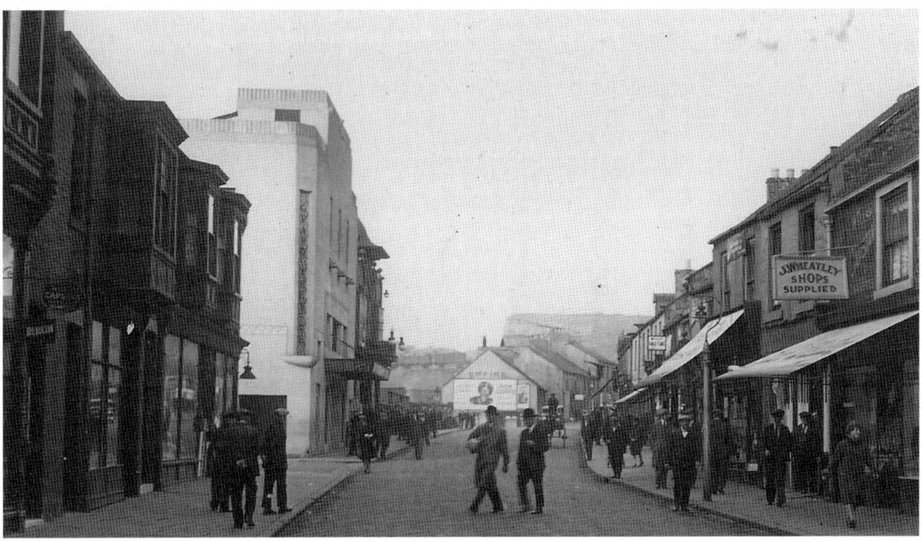

Another view of the north section of Newbottle Street, seen here in the 1940s, with Table Rock visible in the distance. Coal trucks from Houghton Colliery can also be seen on a siding in the background.

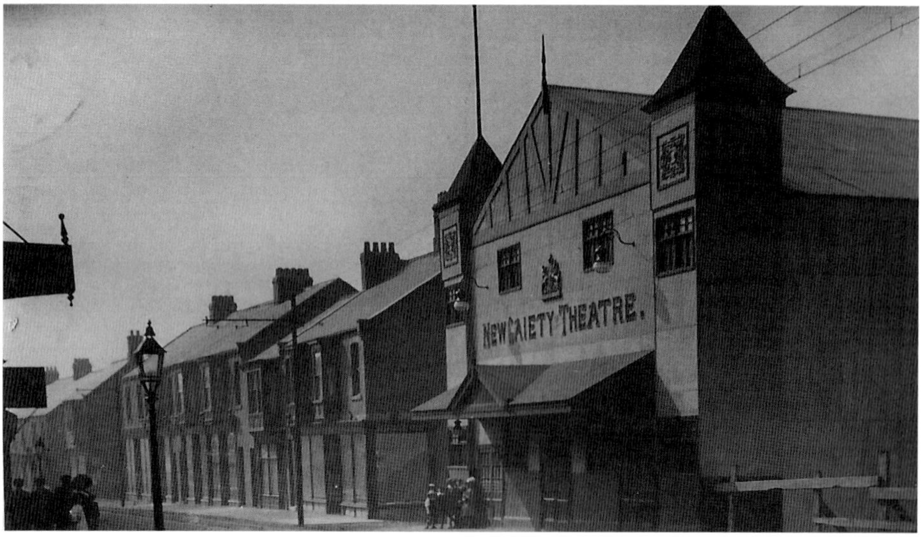

The New Gaiety Theatre on Newbottle Street, circa 1910. In 1925 the name was changed to the Grand, but four years later it closed down and was demolished. On April 21st 1930, a new theatre opened on the site and was known as the New Grand Theatre. This theatre closed in March 1975 and was converted into a supermarket.

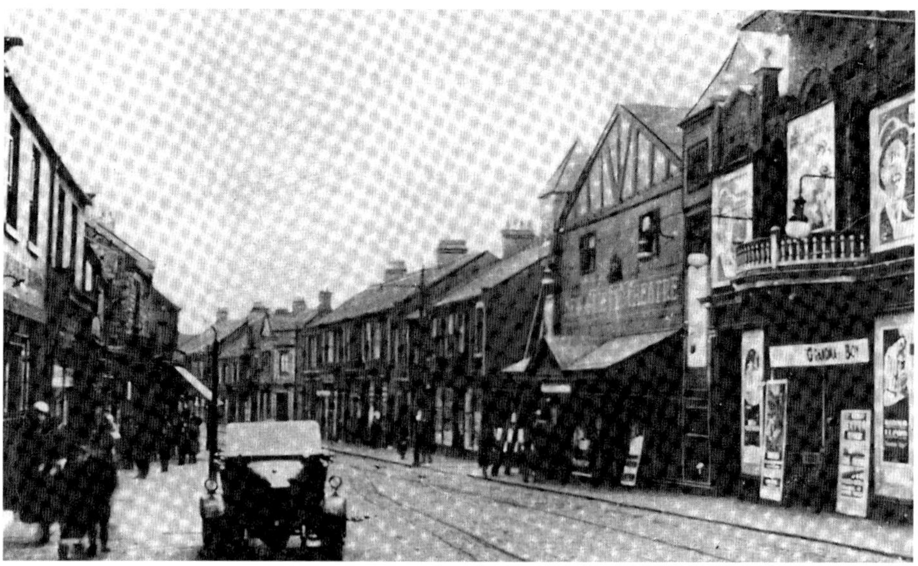

The Empire Theatre alongside the Gaiety on Newbottle Street, circa 1920s. The Empire opened in August 1911 and was in use for many years until it was converted into a bingo hall in 1961. The building was gutted and rebuilt as Empire House in 2000 and is currently occupied by Houghton Dance Academy and also Houghton Carpet Centre.

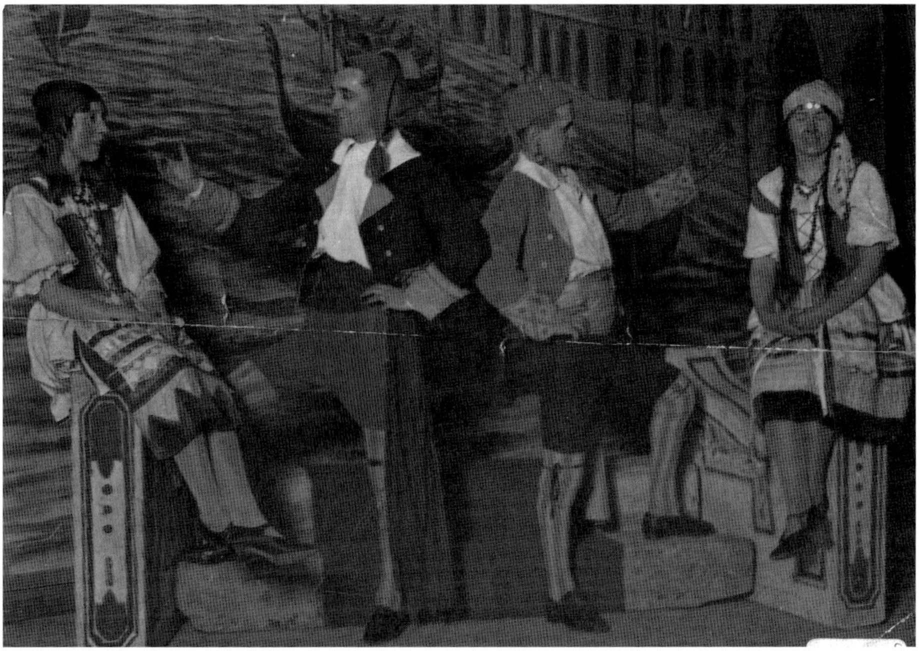

The players on stage in the New Grand Theatre during the first performance at the new venue, Easter 1930. The first show was The Gondoliers, a popular comic opera by Gilbert and Sullivan.

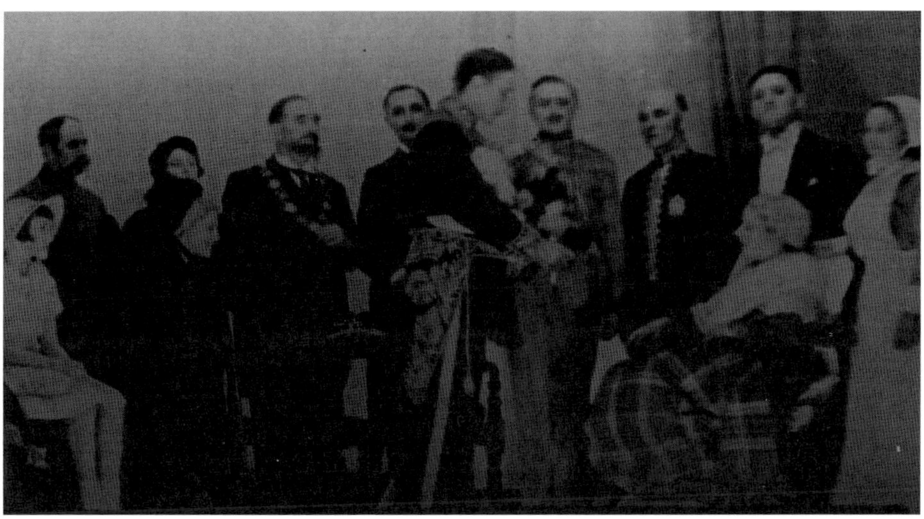

Another view of a production inside one of Houghton's theatres on Newbottle Street. Can anyone identify the show and venue?

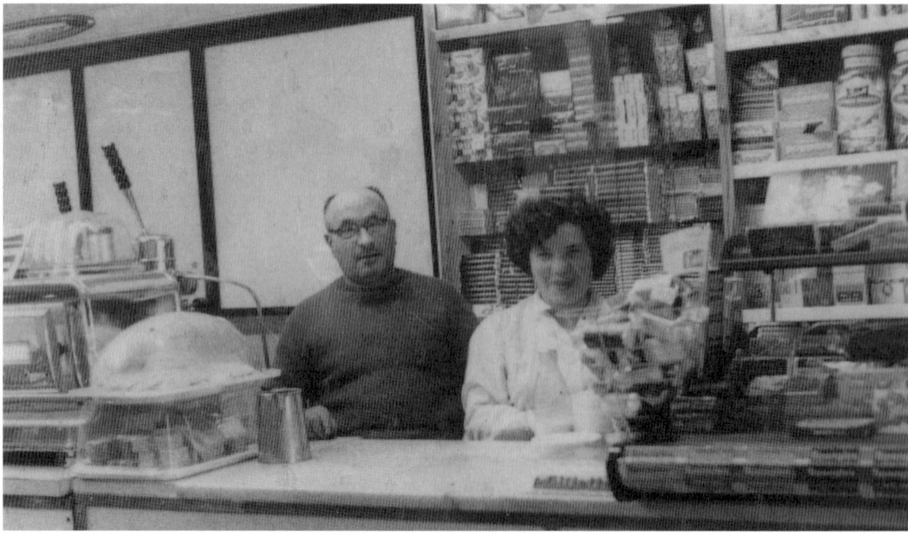

No visit to Newbottle Street would be complete without calling into one of the ice cream parlours. Pictured above is an interior view of the Roma Cafe, 15 Newbottle Street, with Diamond Jaconelli and his niece Edvige Gallone, circa 1950s. Mr Jaconelli brought Edvige and her sister Iolanda over from Valvori, Italy, to work in the shop. They remained loyal employees until his retirement when they purchased the ice cream business from him.

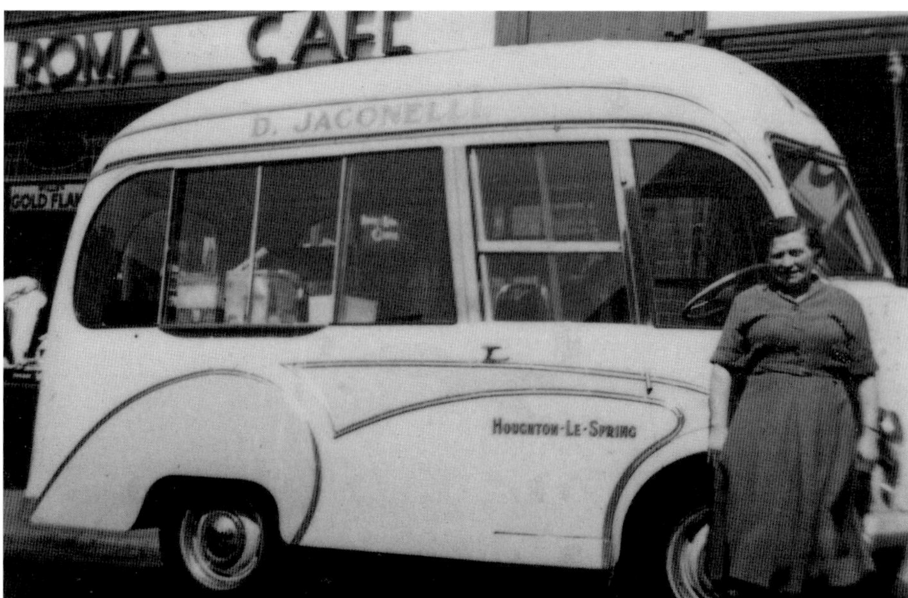

Mrs Lena Jaconelli poses with a new ice cream van outside the Roma Cafe, circa 1950s. The cafe was in Jubilee House, which replaced the demolished Royal Oak Inn in 1935. In more recent times this site was the location of Woolworths.

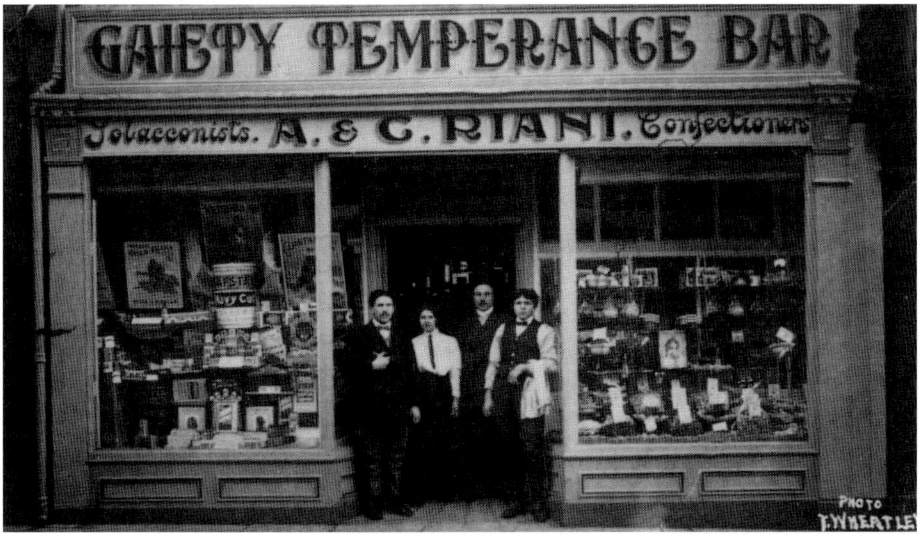

Allessandro and Columbo Riani stand outside their business premises, the Gaiety Temperance Bar at 67 Newbottle Street, circa 1912. The cousins originated from Castelnuovo di Garfagnana, in the Lucca Province, Tuscany, Italy, and had come to Houghton in the early 1900s. Their first business was based at 20 Sunderland Street.

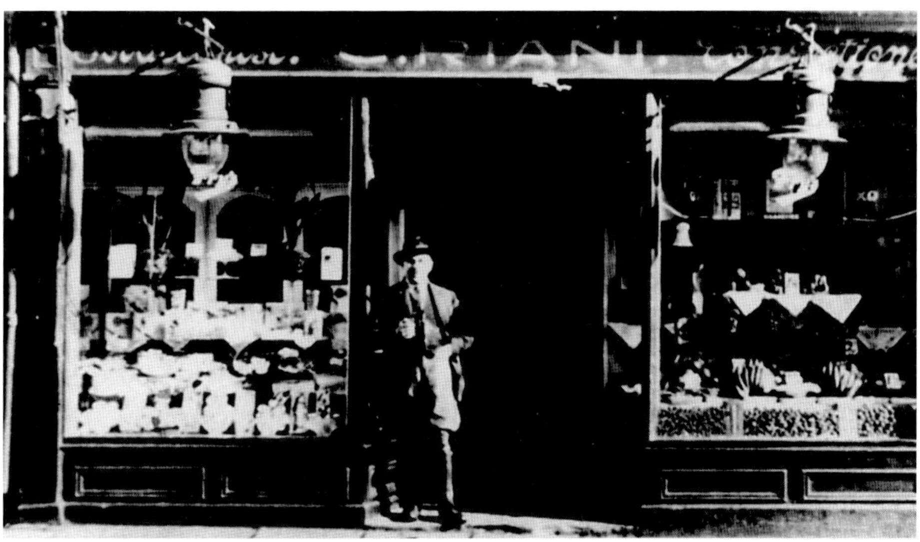

Columbo Riani outside his shop in the late 1920s. Sadly, his cousin and partner Allessandro had been killed during the Great War. The business continued to operate from these premises until its closure in the early 1990s.

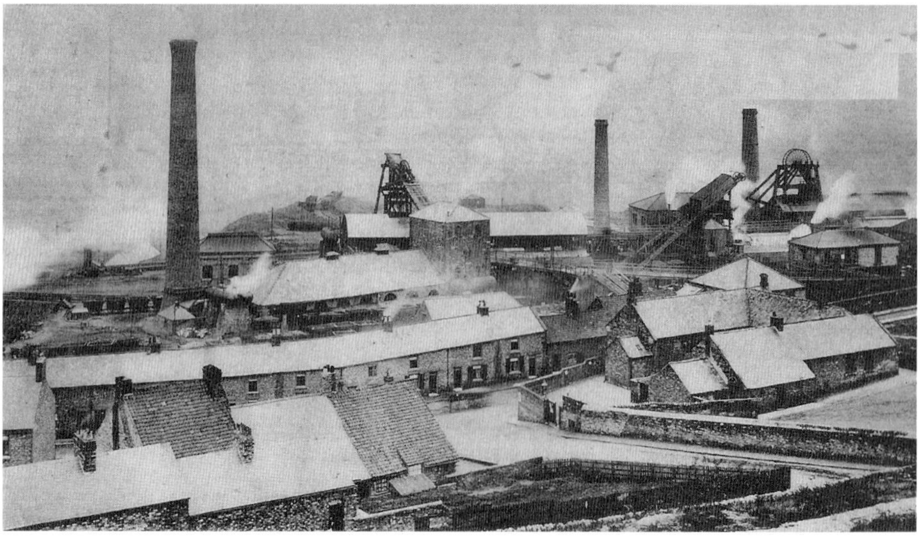

A view from the hillside of the bank top and workings of Houghton Colliery, circa 1900. Work had started on the sinking of the pit on April 29th 1823 and the shaft was completed to the Hutton seam in 1827.

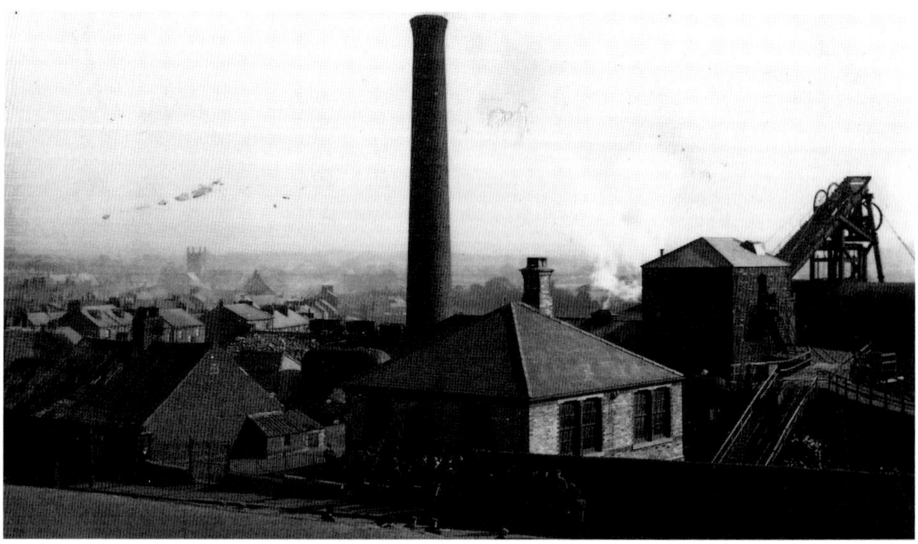

Miners waiting outside the office of Houghton Colliery on Newbottle Lane, circa 1895. The colliery closed in 1981, the last underground shift being completed on Thursday September 24th.

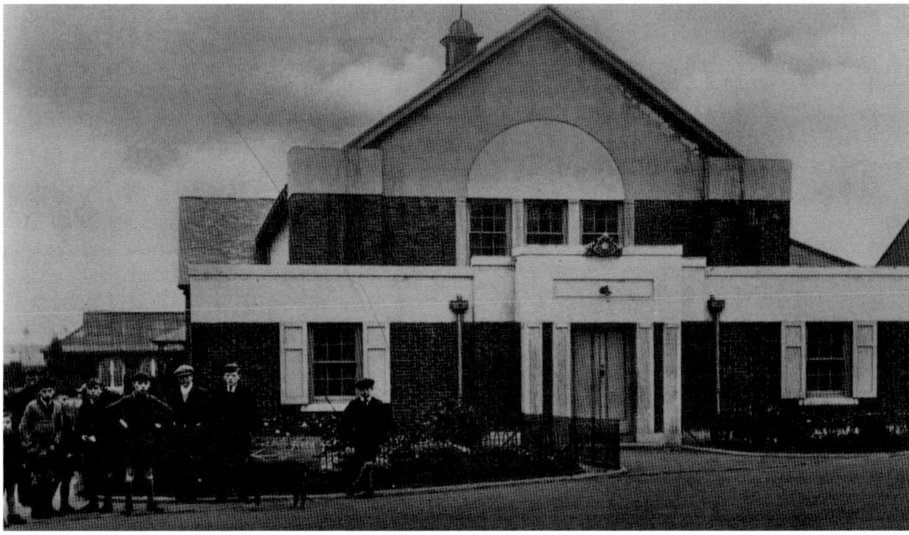

A group of young lads pose outside the Colliery Welfare Hall, circa 1935. The Hall opened in 1931 and accompanied a bowling green, tennis courts and bandstand which had been erected several years earlier for the use of Houghton's miners.

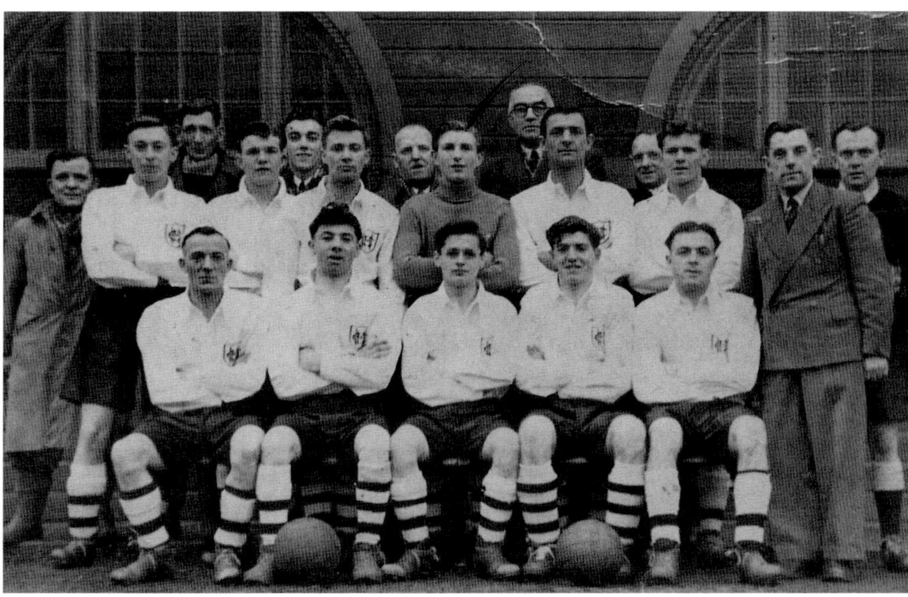

Houghton Colliery Mechanics football team in front of the Colliery Welfare sports pavilion, circa 1953. The players wearing strips are: Front Row - Bobby Patrick; Norman Wardle; Len Gibson; Tommy Smith; and George Edwards. Middle Row - Ron Adey; Bobby Thompson; Billy Besford; George Davison (goal keeper); Wilf Bassett; and Jim Skinner.

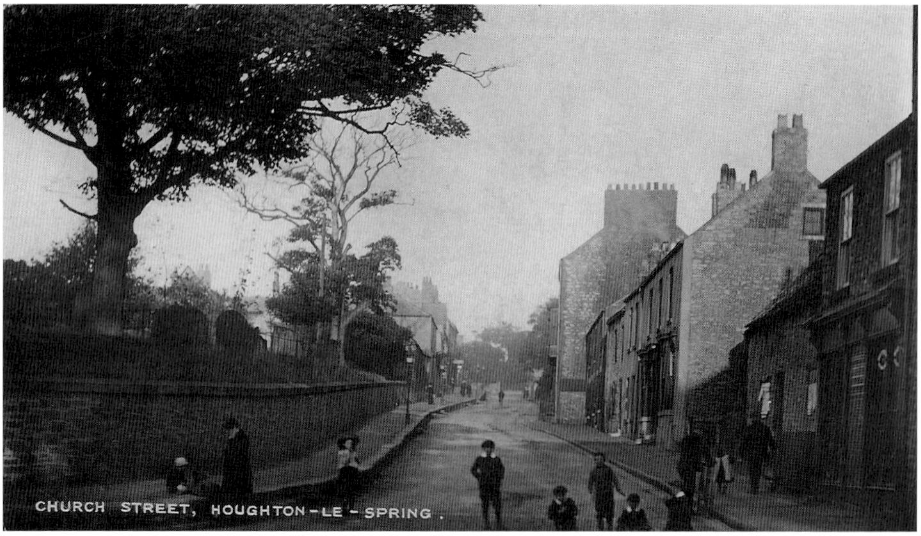

Children playing at the lower end of Church Street around 1905. A central section of the street was demolished in the 1960s. Many of the remaining properties on the street, which was originally known as Commons Lane, date from the early 1800s.

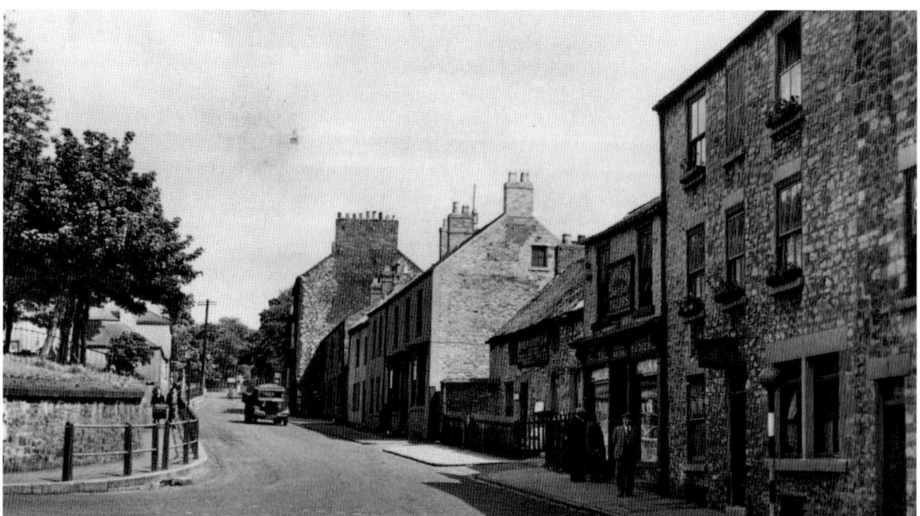

A similar view of Church Street in the 1930s. The Red Lion Inn, one of Houghton's oldest public houses, can be seen on the right. This pub is mentioned in a 1798 guide book of crossroads as being one of the main Postal Inns from which riders and coaches conveyed both mail and passengers. The pub closed in 1975 and is now occupied by an estate agency and solicitors practice.

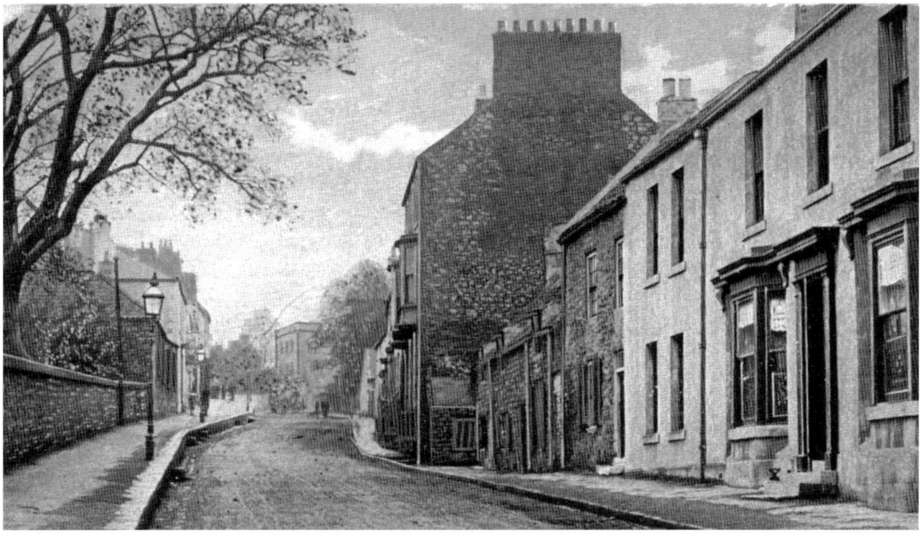

Looking east up Church Street around 1900. The large gable end of Glendale House, 10 Church Street, can be seen in the centre of the photograph, with a glimpse of Houghton Hall in the distance. In recent years work has been carried out on the lower end of the street to give it a traditional appearance.

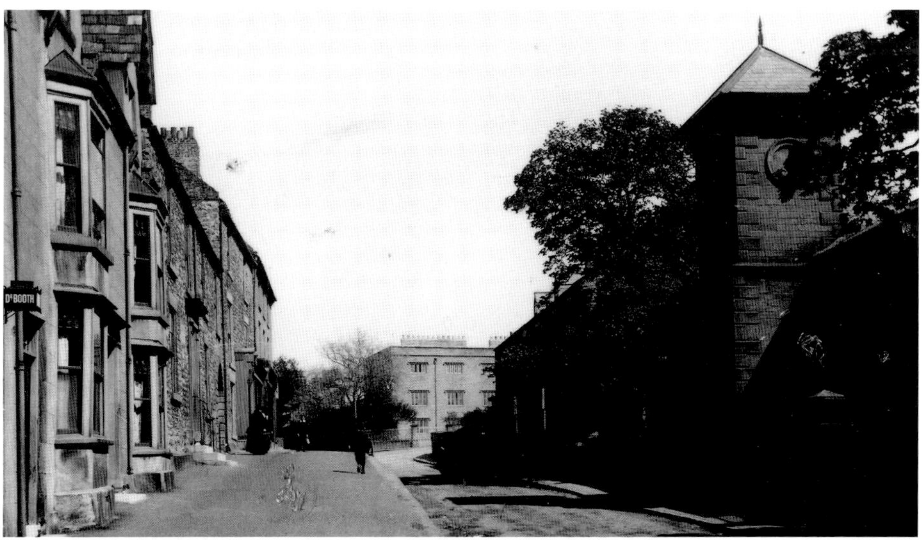

This raised section of Church Street, seen circa 1895, was known as The Quay. Over the years The Quay was occupied by a range of shops and businesses, including the Council Rates Department, a chemist, a newsagent, a public library, the original YMCA and several residential properties. On November 24th 1912, a portion of Dawson's chemists was destroyed by a huge fire which could be seen across the district. The tramway's takings were boosted by sightseers that night!

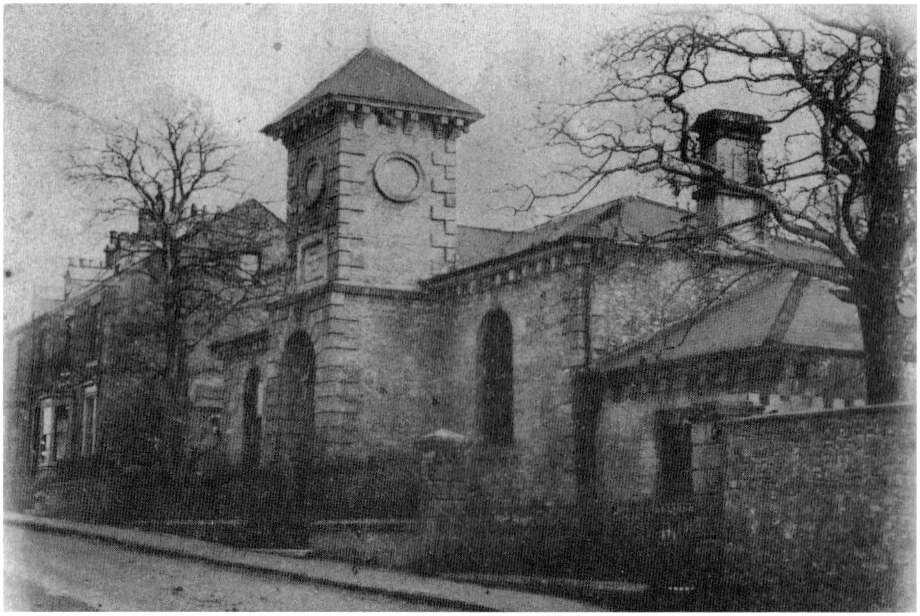

The Mechanics Institute on Church Street, seen above around 1895, opened in 1852 and featured a library of 800 books. In 1881 it became known as the Church Institute & Reading Rooms. The building was demolished in the 1960s to make way for the A690 dual-carriageway.

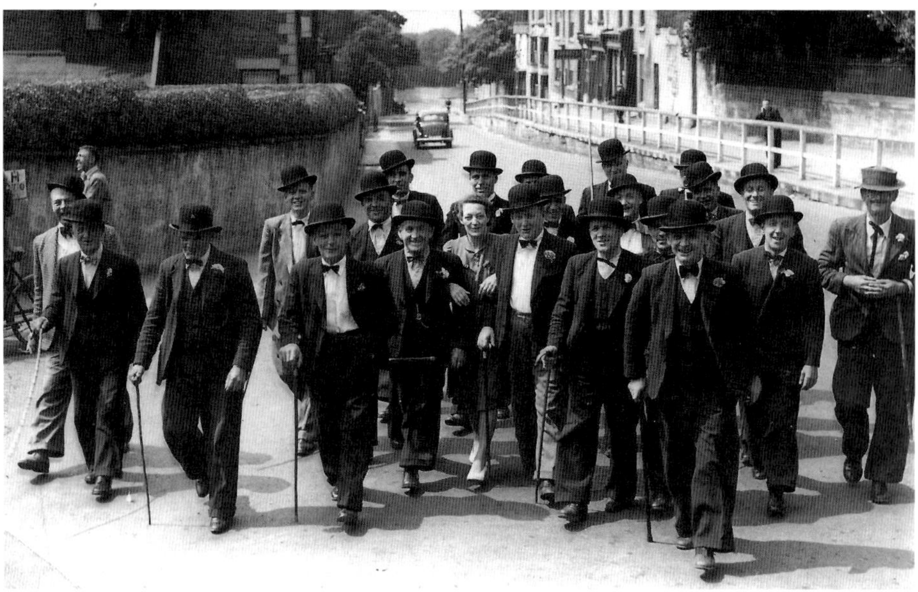

Thomas Forester, second left, and friends head up Church Street on their return to Houghton Social Club after a jolly boys outing in the 1950s. At this time the Club was housed in Houghton Hall.

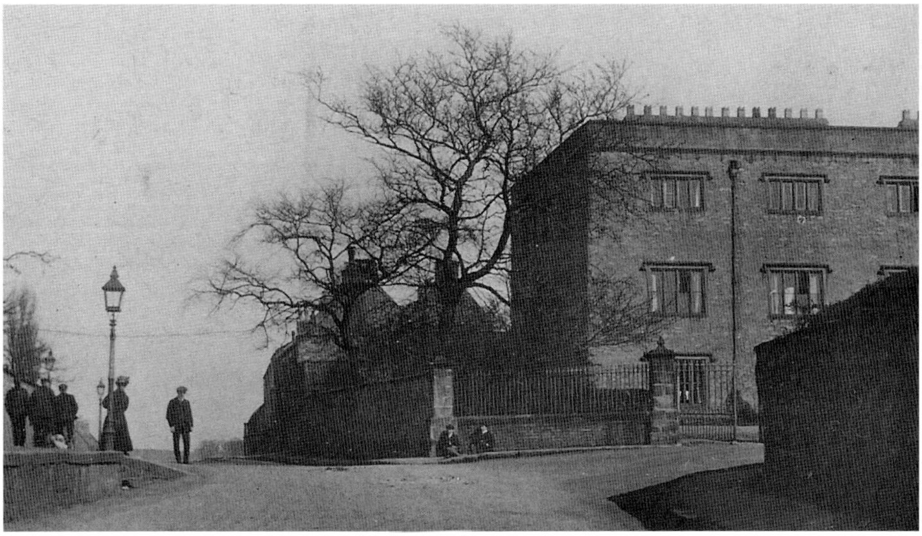

Houghton Hall, seen here on the right in 1895, is thought to have been built by Robert Hutton who was Rector of Houghton from 1589 until 1623. The Hutton family sold the Hall in 1839 and its ownership passed through the hands of many noteworthy residents, including Sir George Elliot, Bart.

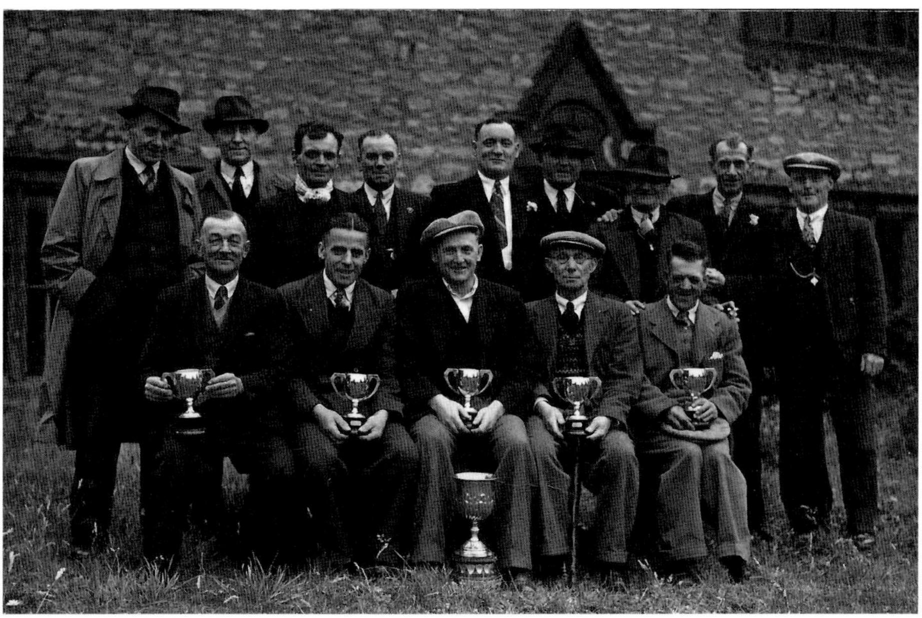

Trophy winners in the grounds of Houghton Social Club in the 1950s. The old Hall was in use as a club between 1917 and 1965. It was officially opened as a YMCA on June 10th 1972 and was in use as such until the 1990s when it was vacated and boarded up. In recent years the Hall has thankfully been restored and renovated and is now a private residence.

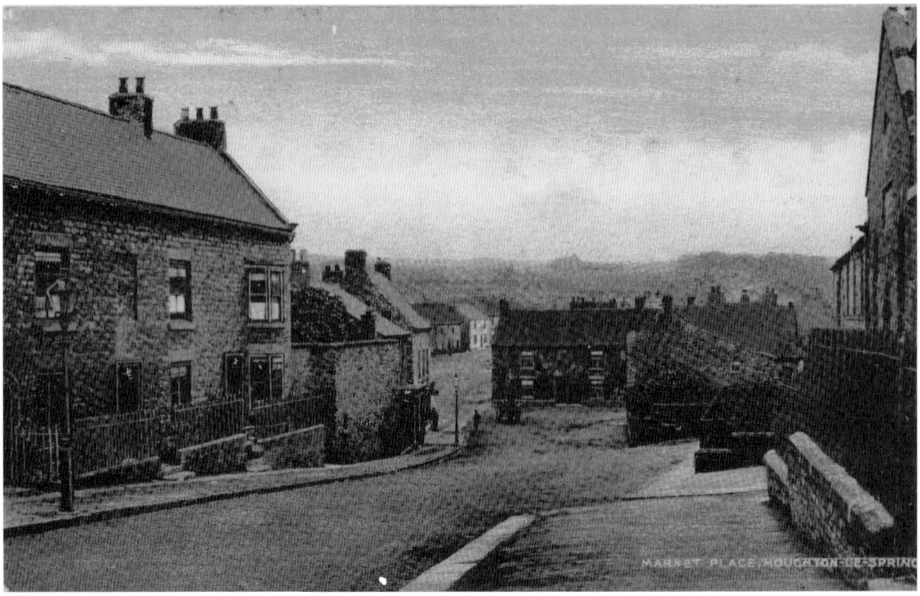

The houses of Nesham Place slope down towards the Market Place, shown here in 1906. This area of Houghton was known as Quality Hill, owing to the grand style of the houses and the occupations of the residents.

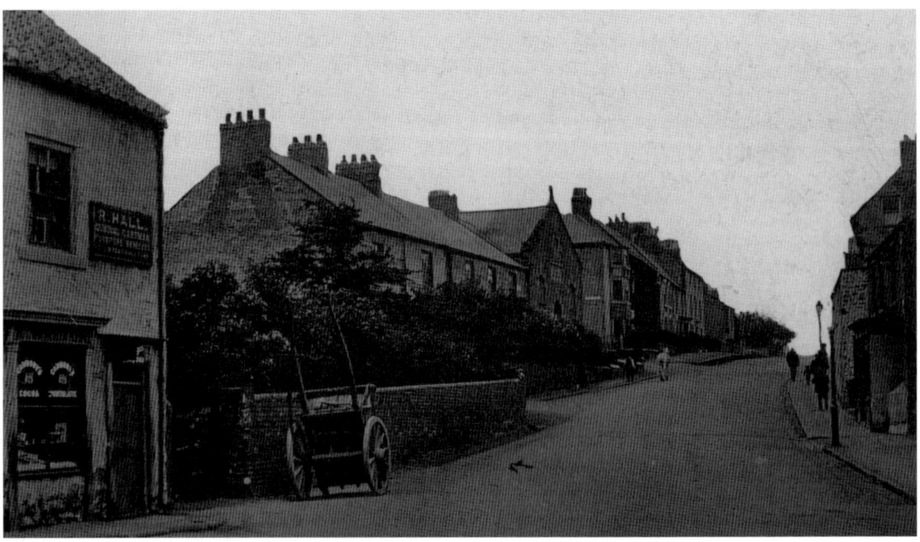

Nesham Place in the 1920s. The sign above the shop on the left advertises the services of R. Hall, a general cartman (*'furniture removed on reasonable terms'*) while R. Walton's shop underneath clearly sells Cadbury's cocoa. The Nesham Place Methodist Church, which closed on September 21st 1980, can be seen in the centre. After demolition the land lay unused for many years before a private dwelling house was erected on the site.

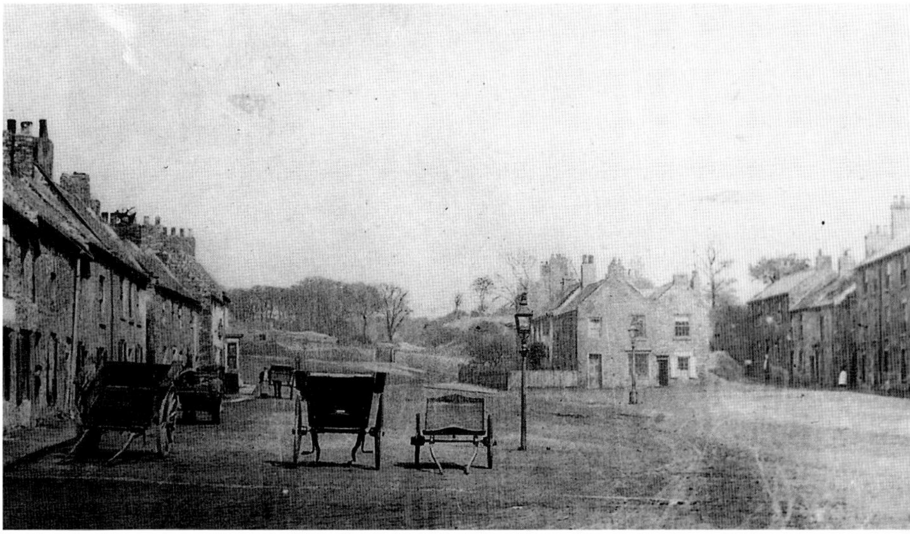

Looking east across Houghton's Market Place, circa 1895. This was the location of the original Saxon Burh, a fortified village close to the water source that is Houghton Burn. The double-gabled house in the centre of the photograph, Elm Place, is thought to have been the location of Houghton Manor House, home to the Le Springs.

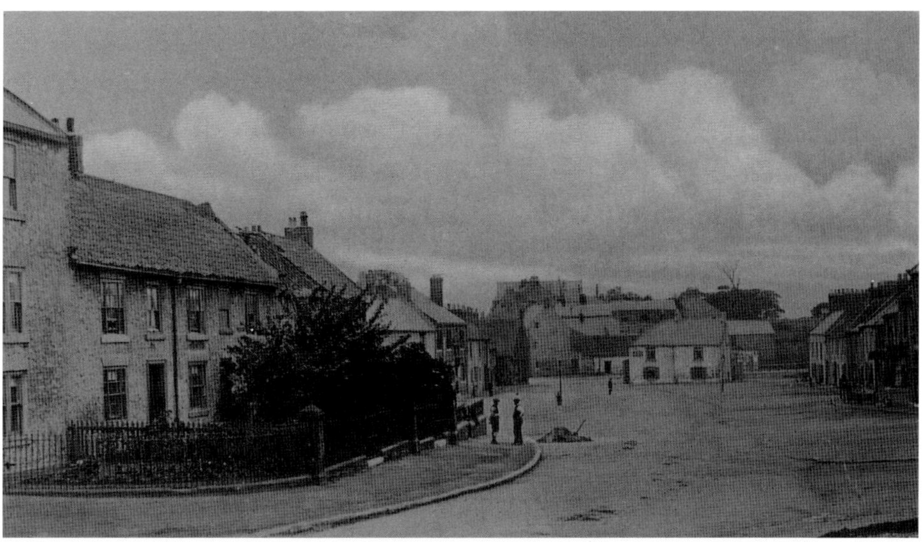

A couple of labourers take a break from shoveling horse manure in Houghton's Market Place around 1910. The stream from the Saxon village, which was culverted, runs behind the houses on the right towards the area known as the Lake.

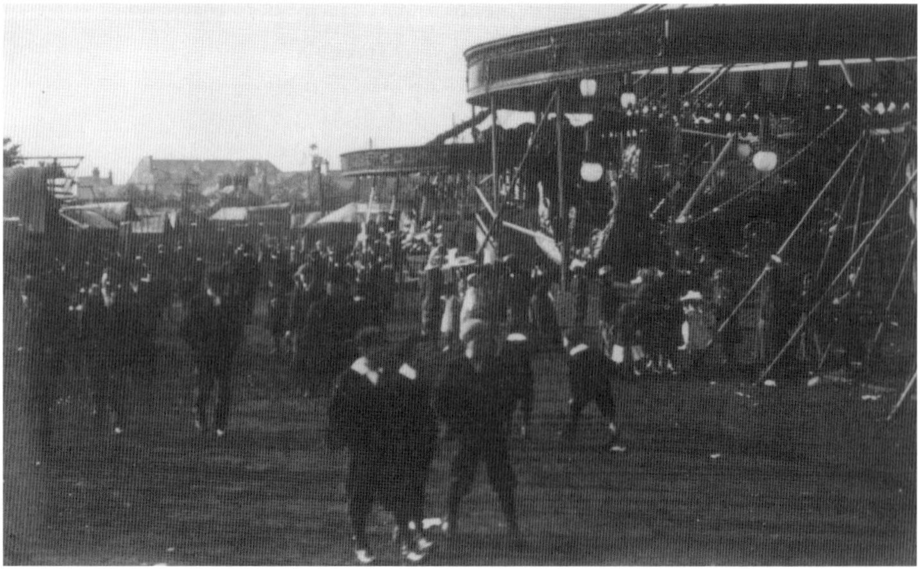

Three young lads stroll around the Lake fairground at Houghton Feast, circa 1895. The festival has its origins over 800 years ago as Michaelmas, the dedication festival of St Michael & All Angels Church. The Lake site was so-called because it was a Victorian pleasure lake in the 1880s.

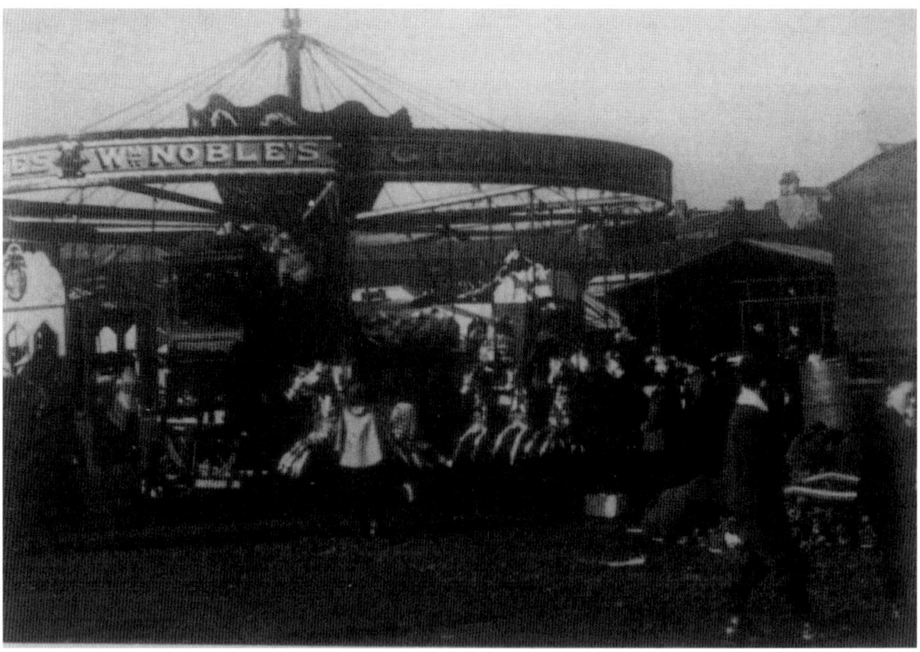

Another early view of the Houghton Feast Lake fairground, circa 1895, featuring William Noble's set of Dobbies, a hand or steam powered forerunner of the galloping horses. Members of the Noble family still attend the Houghton Feast fairground to this day, which has been housed on the Rectory Field, Dairy Lane, since 1968.

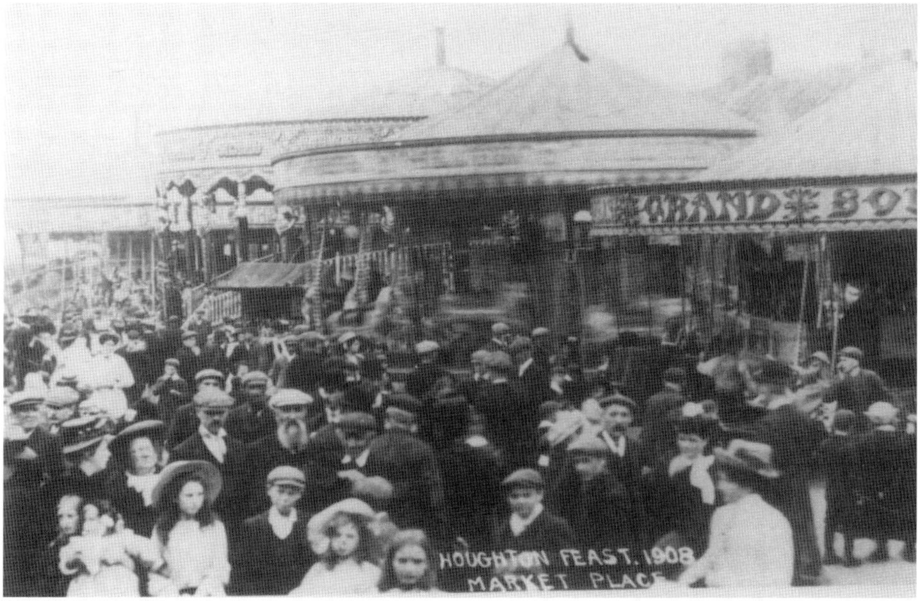

A packed view of the Houghton Feast fairground in the Market Place in 1908. Ralph & Pedley's switchback ride can be seen to the left, while to the right is a set of Dobbies with 'Grand South Africa' on the rounding boards.

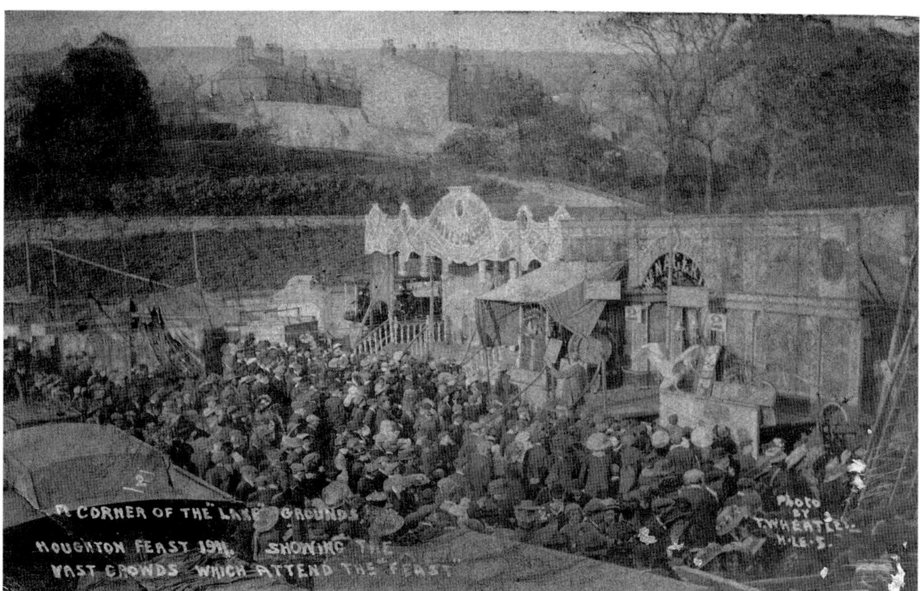

A rare view of the packed Lake fairground at Houghton Feast in 1911. Mrs Elizabeth Paine's Bioscope Show can be seen to the left, with Manders' Menagerie to the right. Admission was 2d and offered the folk of Houghton a rare chance to see live, wild animals.

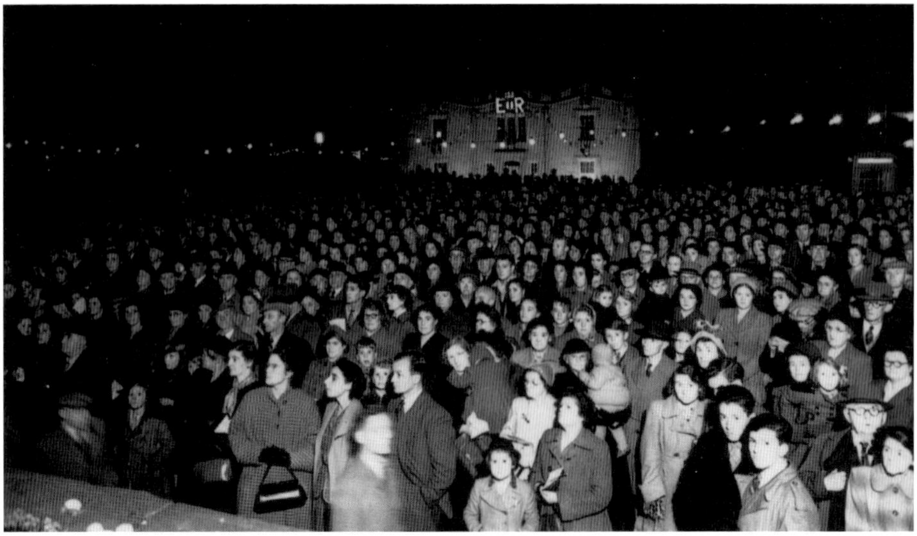

Hymn singers in the Broadway on Houghton Feast Sunday, October 1953. The outdoor hymn singing event was initiated by Rector Oswald Noel Gwilliam in 1949 and soon became a staple attraction of the Feast with thousands in attendance each year.

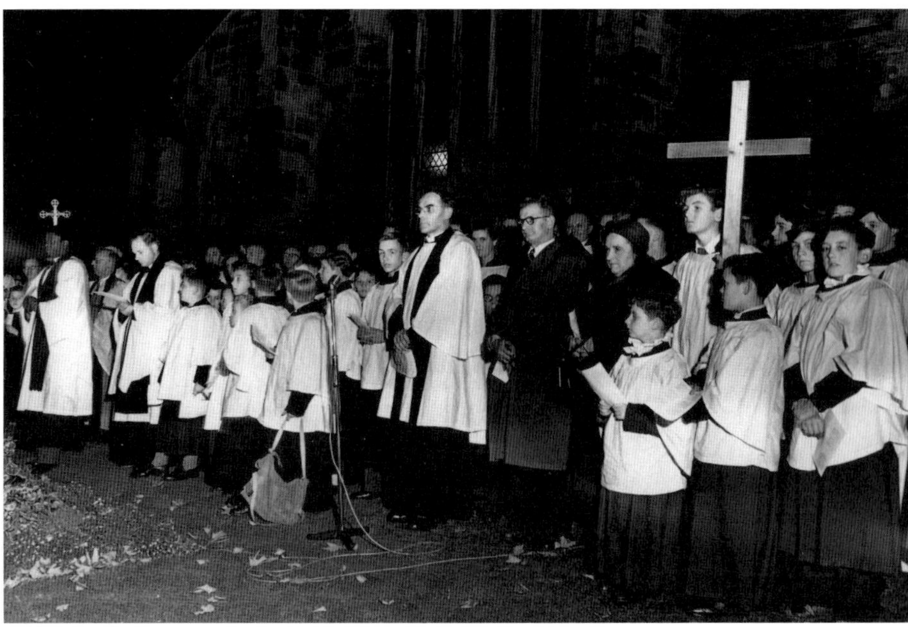

Members of the clergy and choir lead the Houghton Feast hymn singing from the lawn in front of St Michael's Church, October 6th 1957. Pictured with the choir, from left, are: Rev Thompson of Nigeria; Rev Peter Sanderson, Curate; Rector O. N. Gwilliam; and Mr Bircham, Chairman of Houghton Urban District Council.

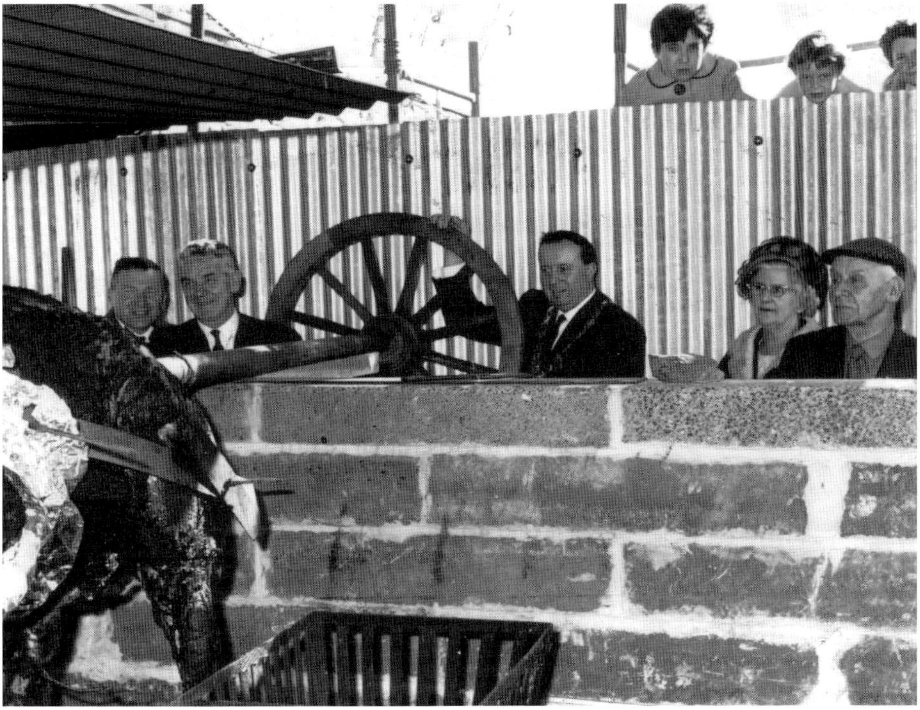

Three young scamps look down on the roasting ox at Houghton Feast 1967, as John Mawston, Chairman of Houghton Urban District Council, turns the spit. Accompanying Mr Mawston at the revived ox roasting, from left, are: Bill Curry, butcher; Walter Winship, baker; Mrs Pearl Mawston; and an unidentified gentleman.

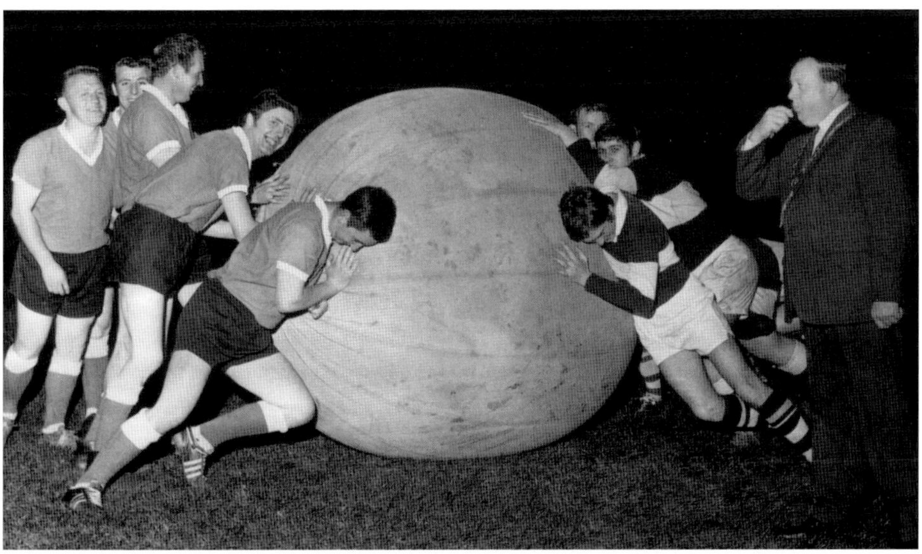

John Mawston referees the Houghton Feast pushball contest at Houghton Rugby Club, October 1967. This contest was just one event of the many that were introduced at the 1967 revival of Houghton Feast. It ended in a draw.

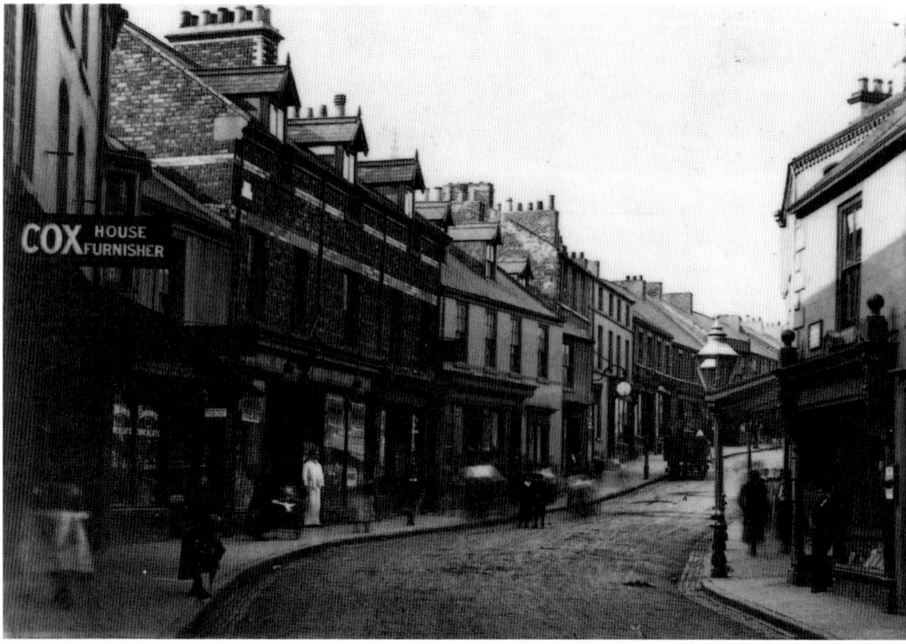

The lower end of Sunderland Street, circa 1895. This street wound its way up from Houghton centre towards the Cut at the north. The lower half was mainly shops and businesses, with the upper half being mainly residential.

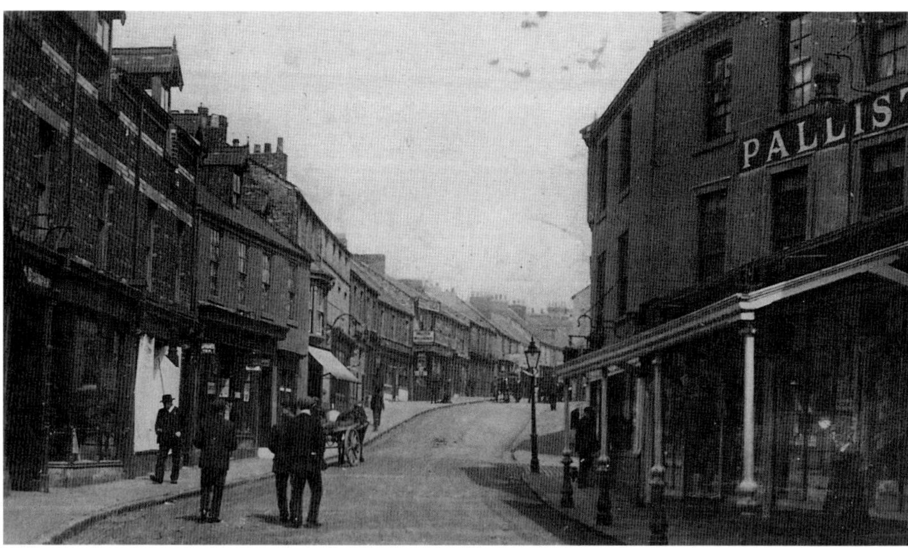

A similar view of Sunderland Street, circa 1900, with Pallisters Store on the right. This once impressive street is now a cul-de-sac and the remaining buildings are now a shadowy reflection of their former proud selves since the A690 dual-carriageway sliced the street apart in the 1960s. Only thirty properties remain from the original street.

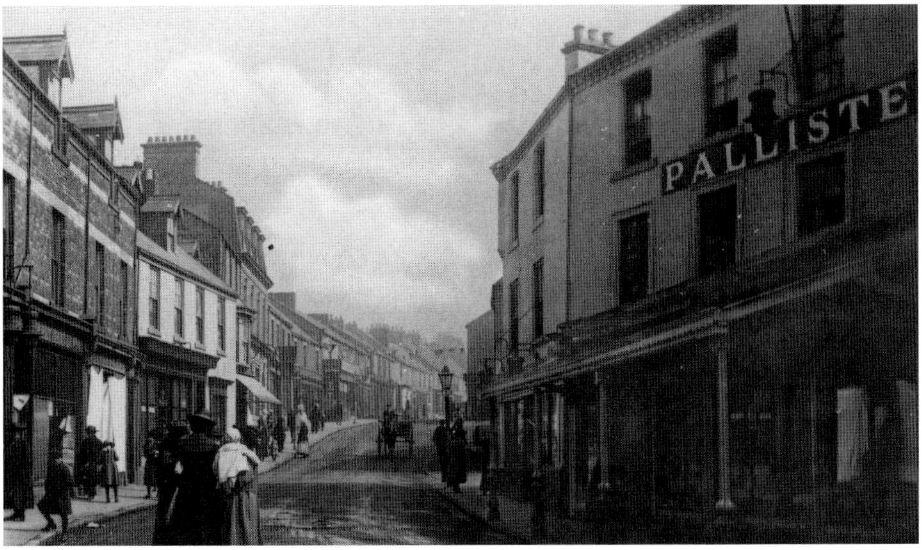

Another early view of the lower end of Sunderland Street, circa 1915. The three storey building on the left side of the street was a branch of the North-Eastern Banking Company, known as Martins Bank in the 1940s. The property has had several recent guises as a wine bar and bistro. These contrasting photos of the street show that the building was heightened at some point.

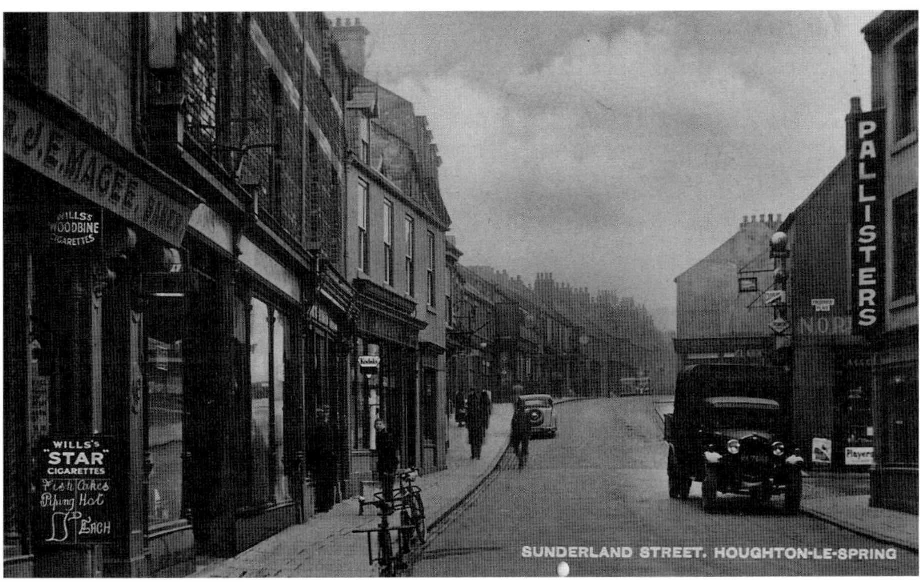

Sunderland Street in the 1930s when the advent of the petrol engine changed the traffic on the street from horse and carts to motor vehicles. Readers will recognise several of the businesses featured in this photograph as they remained on this street for many years.

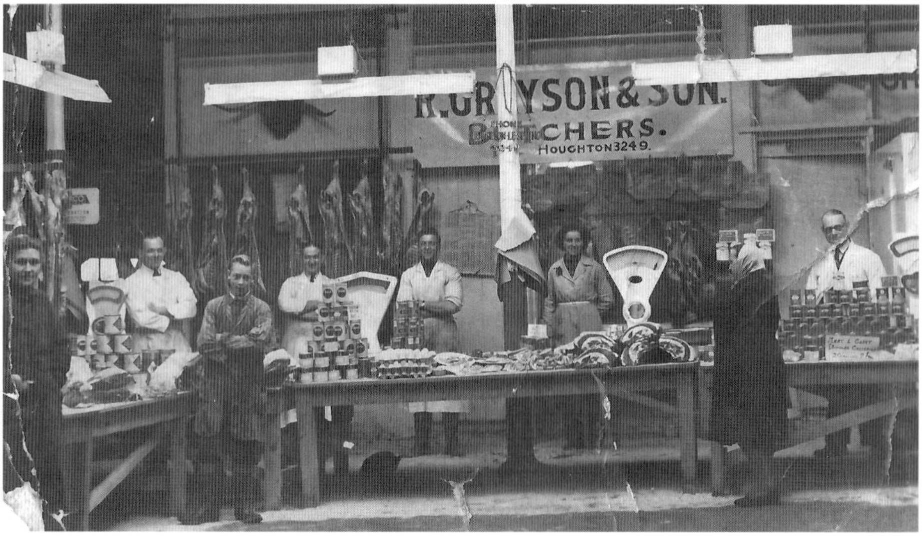

The meat counter of R. Grayson & Son, butchers, in the indoor covered market, circa 1950. The market was located in the Town Hall building and had entrances on Sunderland Street and Newbottle Street. Standing behind the counter, from right, are: Richard Grayson; unidentified lady; Frank Forester; Charlie Grayson Jnr; and Fred Ord. The business operated from the market for many years and moved to Newbottle Street when the Town Hall was demolished in the 1960s.

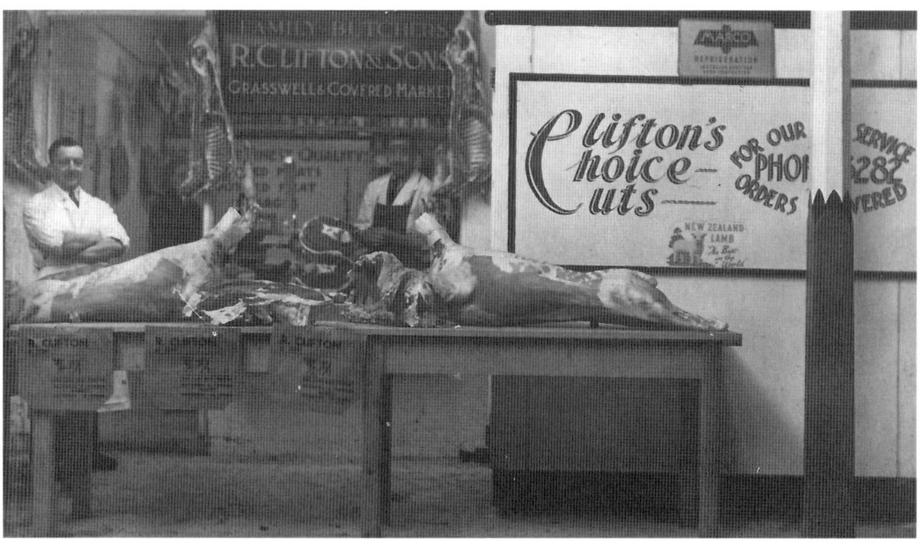

An impressive display of meat on R. Clifton & Sons' stall in the indoor market, circa 1950. Pictured behind the counter is Harry Clifton, left. Butcher Jack Kinmond, seen in the background, was involved with the revival of the Houghton Feast ox roasting in 1967.

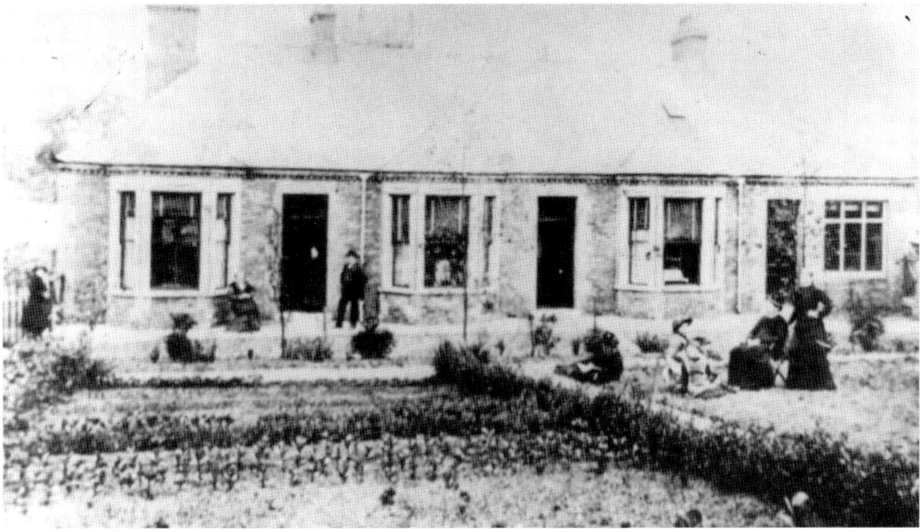

A rare view of Stocksfield Terrace, circa 1890. The terrace consisted of three cottages which were accessed via a small road alongside the Black Lion public house on Sunderland Street. The photograph shows the front of the cottages, with the Lake grounds off to the left. The level at the rear of the properties was much lower and it is thought that the stables and carriages were once housed underneath.

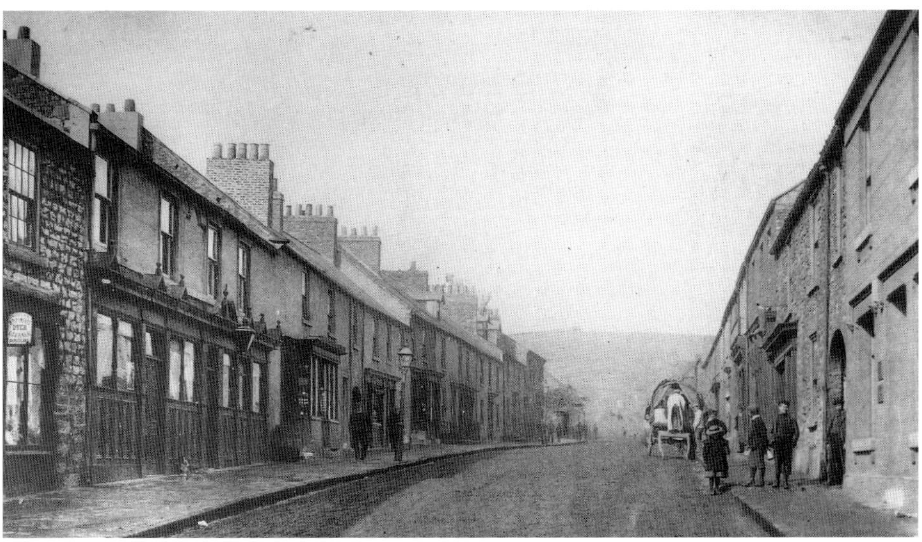

The Queen's Head public house, known locally as the Pillars, at 32 Sunderland Street, can be seen on the left, circa 1899. At this time the landlord, Patrick Henry, was fined £1 and 8 shilling costs for selling adulterated brandy. The pub, which dates back to at least 1824, ceased trading on November 3rd 1958.

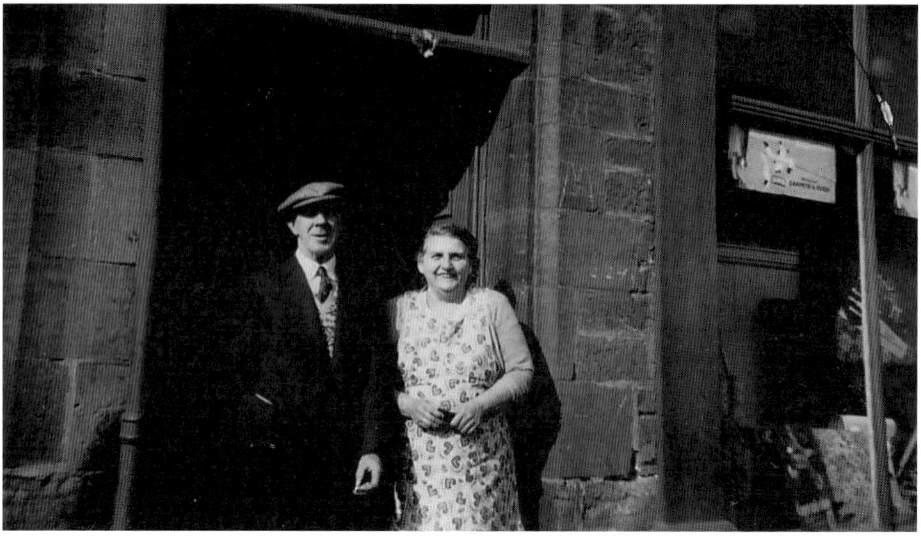

Mr and Mrs Robinson in the doorway of 52 Sunderland Street in 1947. This residential property had a shop attached, the window of which can be seen on the right, and was occupied by the tailoring department of the Co-op. Next door to this was the County Arms public house, which was set slightly further back from the road on the corner of the Mautland Street opening.

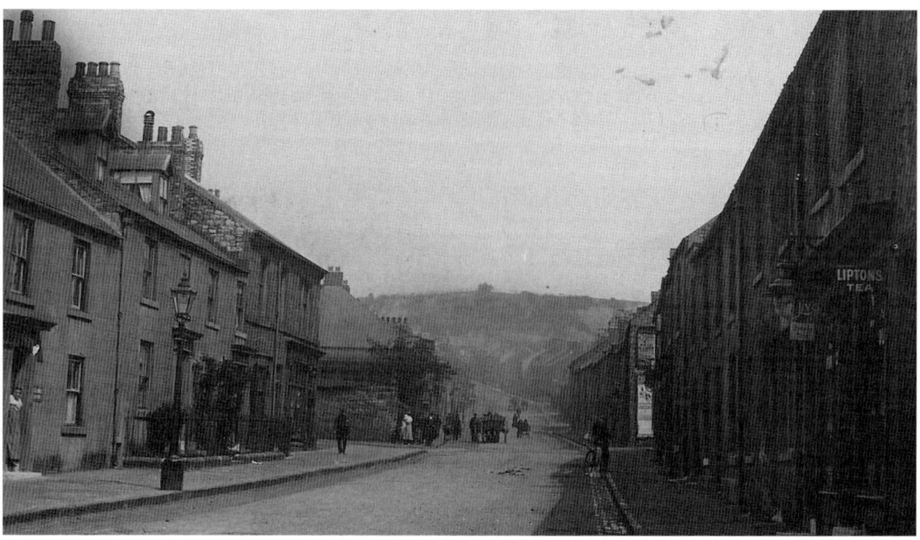

The crossroads on Sunderland Street, circa 1910. Mautland and George Streets were to the left and the Police Station and Workhouse on William Street were to the right. The property on the top left corner of the crossroads was once Hopper House, home to iron founder George Hopper, and became a branch of the Hetton Downs Amicable Industrial Co-operative Society in 1903.

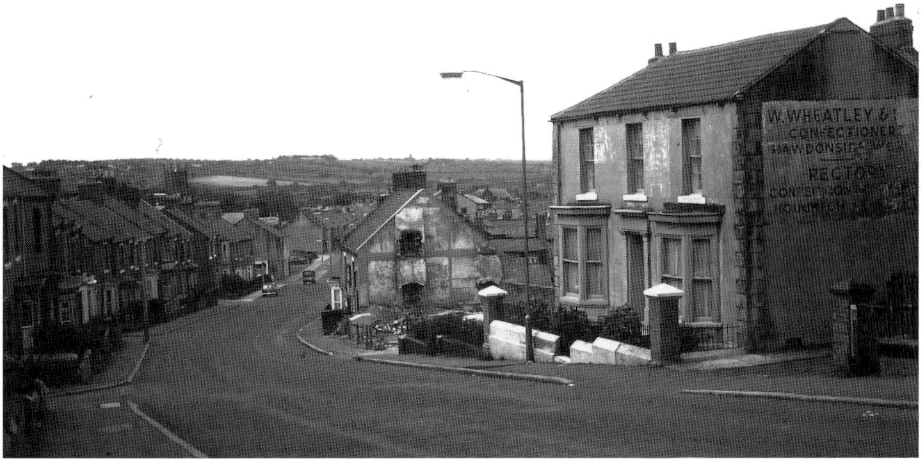

A southerly view of Sunderland Street in 1965, with Wheatley's confectionery factory at Hawdonside Works, right. The confectionery business was founded in 1863 by Crimean War veteran, George Wheatley. At the time of this photograph many of the properties had started to be demolished in preparation for the A690 redevelopments.

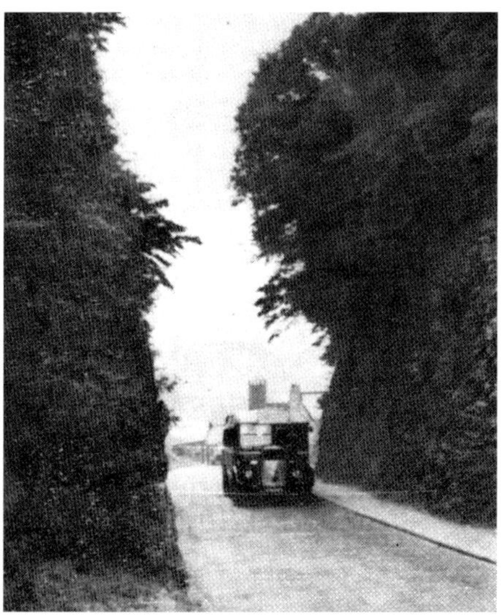

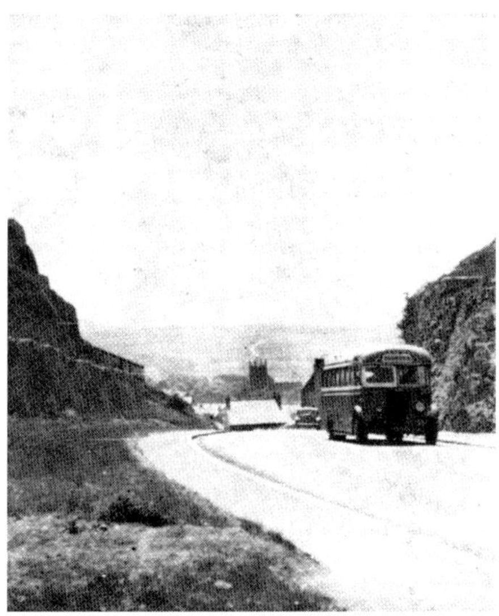

Comparative views of the Cut at the top of Sunderland Street in the 1930s and 1949, right, showing how the opening in the rock has been improved over the years. 50,000 tons of magnesian limestone was excavated from the Cut in the 1930s.

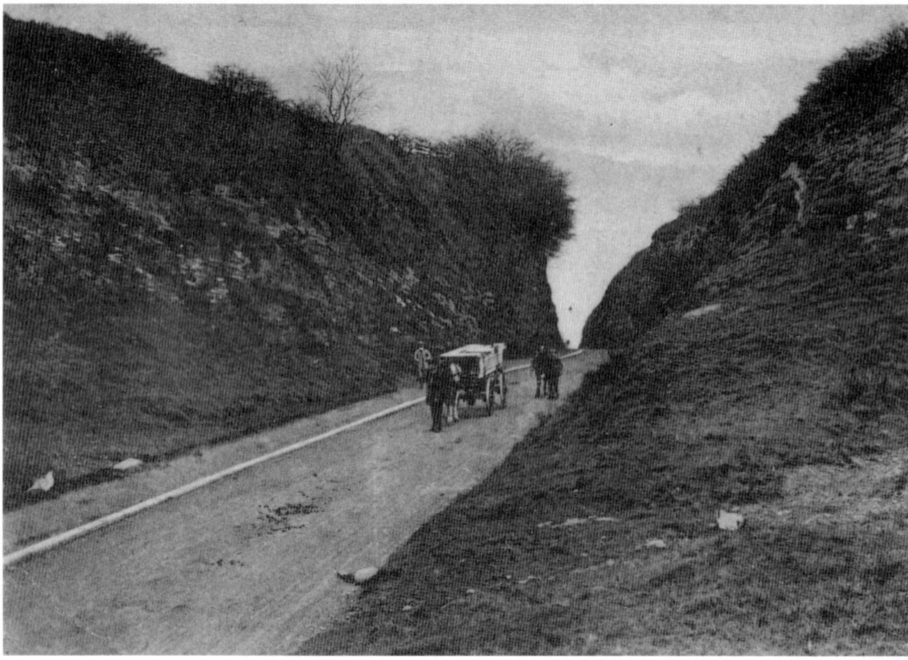

A cartman hesitantly leads his horse and load down the steep road of Houghton Cut, circa 1890. Such a journey would have been treacherous in icy weather. This gap has always existed in the cliffs in some form and it is claimed that it was widened by French prisoners of war during the Napoleonic Wars in 1815.

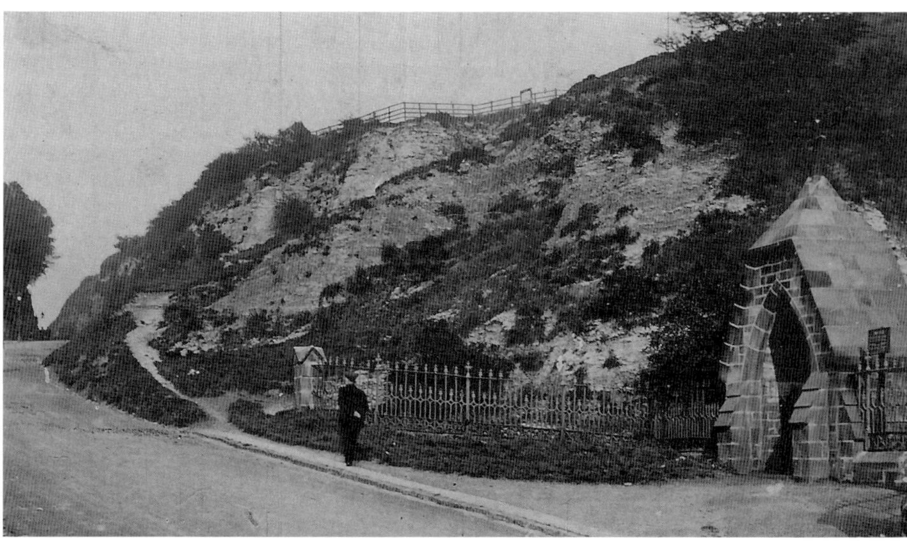

The lych gate of Hillside Cemetery and Houghton Cut, circa 1919. The archway and railings have been restored in recent years at a cost of almost £30,000. On September 4th 2006, the second of two time capsules was interred inside the structure during the rebuilding stage.

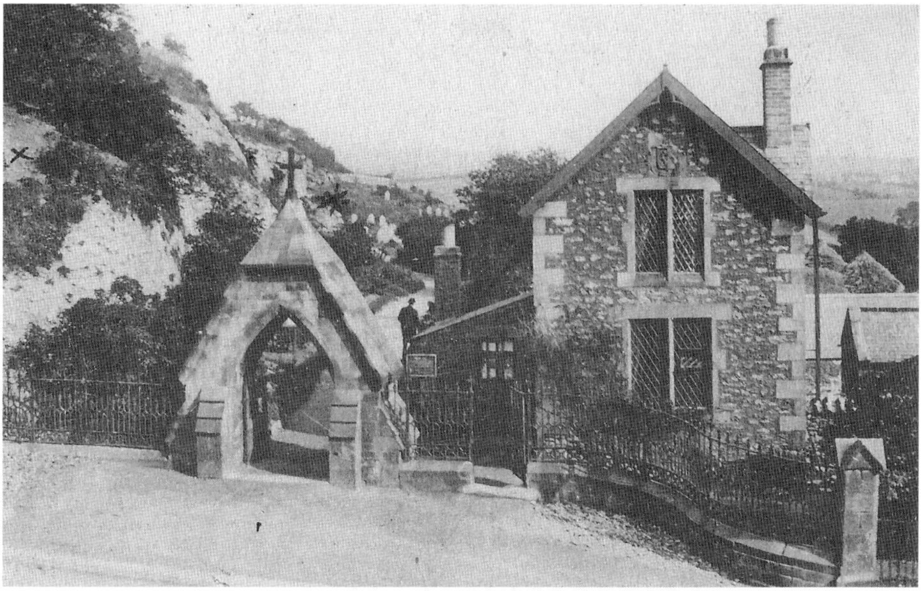

The Hillside Cemetery lych gate and sexton's lodge on Sunderland Street, circa 1898. At the time of the photograph the lodge was occupied by Edwin Place and his wife Margaret. Edwin died in 1932 and was buried at the east end of the burial ground.

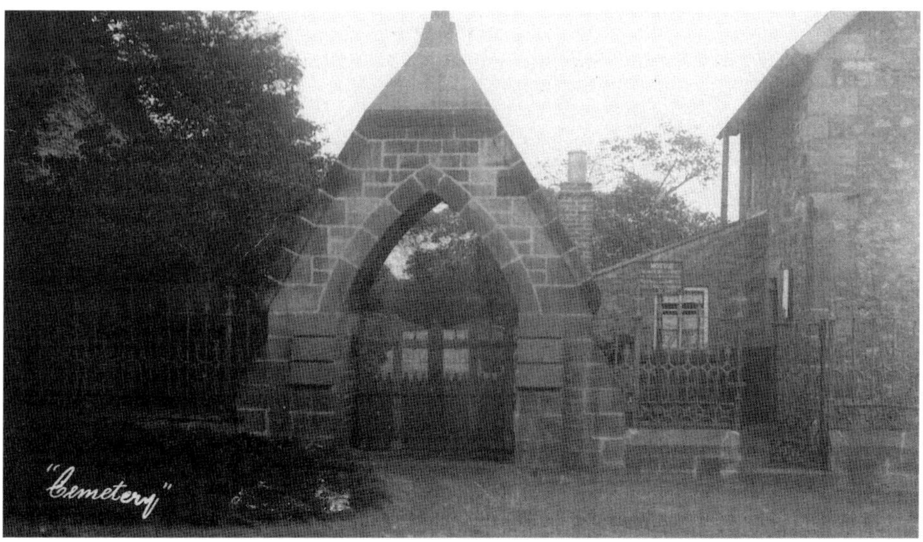

A closer view of the lych gate at the entrance to Hillside Cemetery, circa 1910. The sign at the right of the archway featured information about the burial fees and a reminder that clergy could not perform funerals on a Sunday.

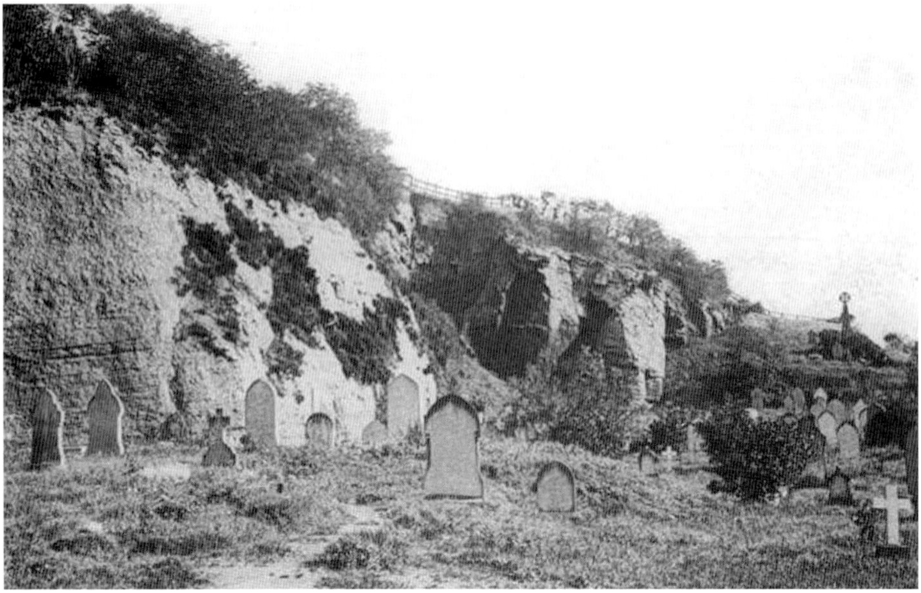

A rare view of the Hillside Cemetery headstones in 1900. The cemetery, which was consecrated on September 4th 1854, was a detached extension to St Michael's churchyard. Rector John Grey's choice of location for the new burial ground was very controversial as the site was once a magnesian limestone rock quarry.

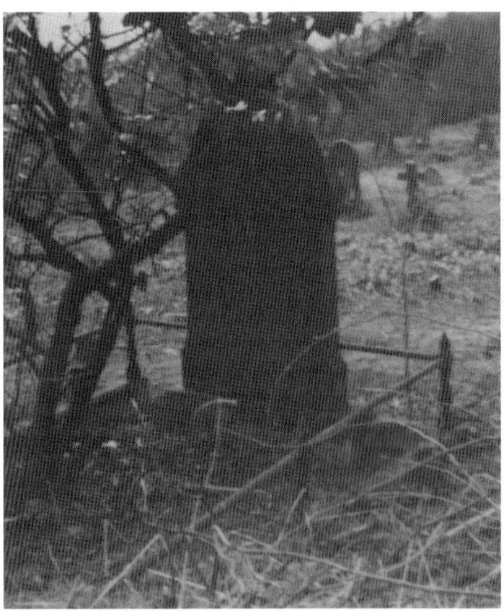

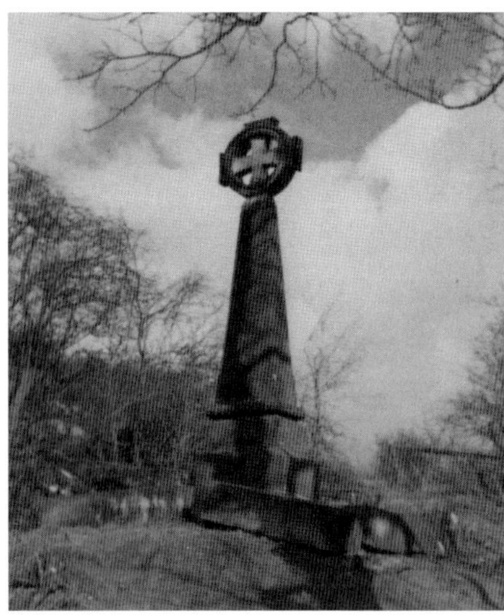

Views of some of the impressive headstones and memorials at Hillside Cemetery in the 1970s. In 1974 the site was cleared and many of the headstones were bulldozed into a corner and buried as part of a clean up operation. It was not until 2005 that the cemetery was closed for new interments.

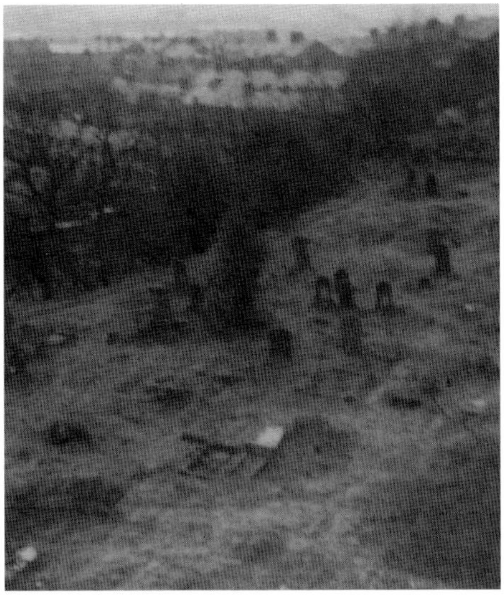

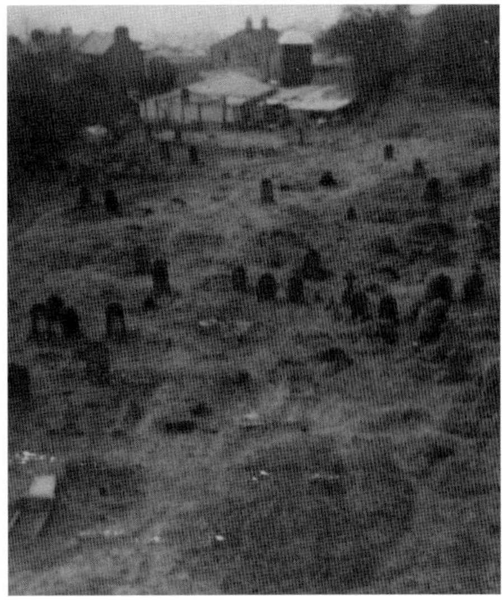

These views of the Hillside Cemetery were taken from the cliff tops in the 1970s and reveal how overgrown the site had become. Many noteworthy residents were interred in the rock face which formed the northern boundary of the burial ground, including: William Standish Standish Esq; Sir George Elliot, Bart.; and General William Beckwith.

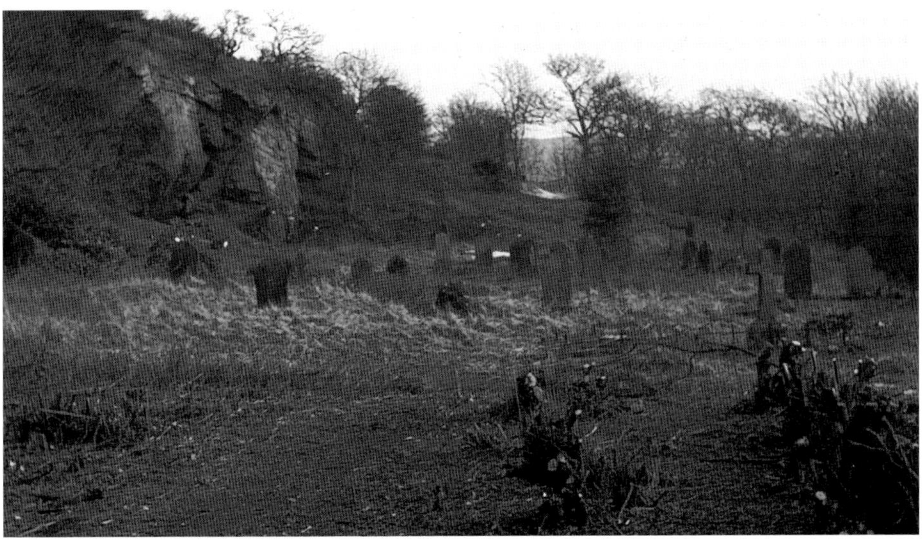

A view of the Hillside Cemetery plateau, circa 1974, prior to it being landscaped. The cruciform memorial to the right is that of Isabella Smyth, landlady of the White Lion public house in the 1890s. The patches of yew trees to the left surround and obscure the pink granite memorial of Rector John Grey, who was interred in his cemetery on November 14th 1895.

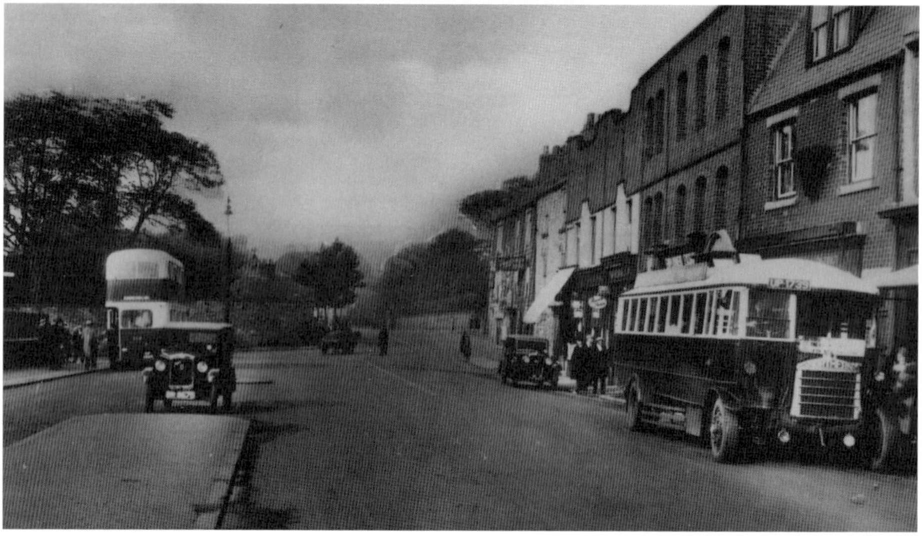

Big Blue Buses at the stand on Durham Road in the 1930s. The Sunderland District Omnibus Company caused a sensation in September 1924 when thirty of the large buses were purchased, signalling the end of its own electric tramway.

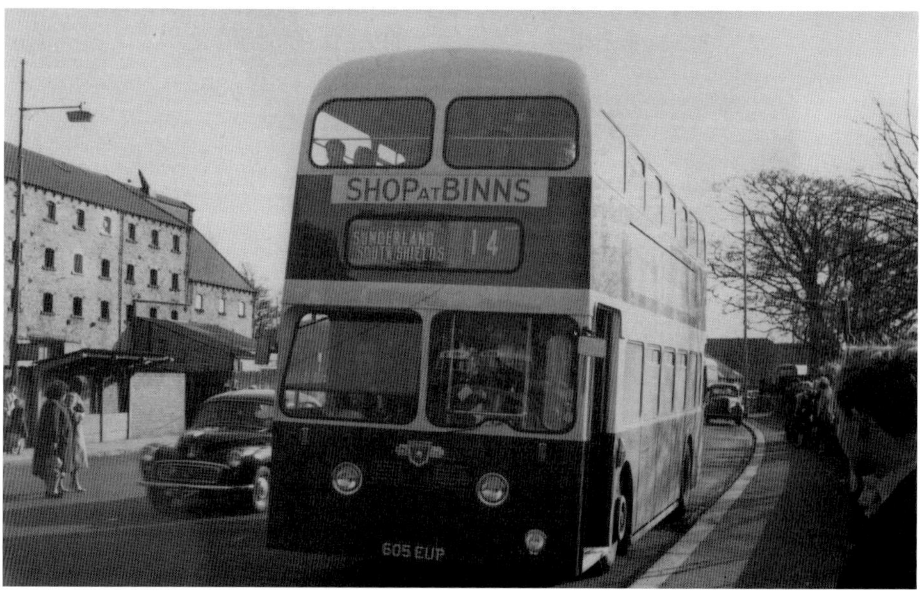

The number 14 South Shields via Sunderland bus passes along Durham Road in the 1950s. The old brewery can be seen in the background. The brewery was founded in 1754 by the Robinson family and was in operation until 1925. It lay dormant for many years before being converted into a nightclub in 1976. The listed building, which suffered fire damage in July 1992, was redeveloped sympathetically into apartments in 1998.

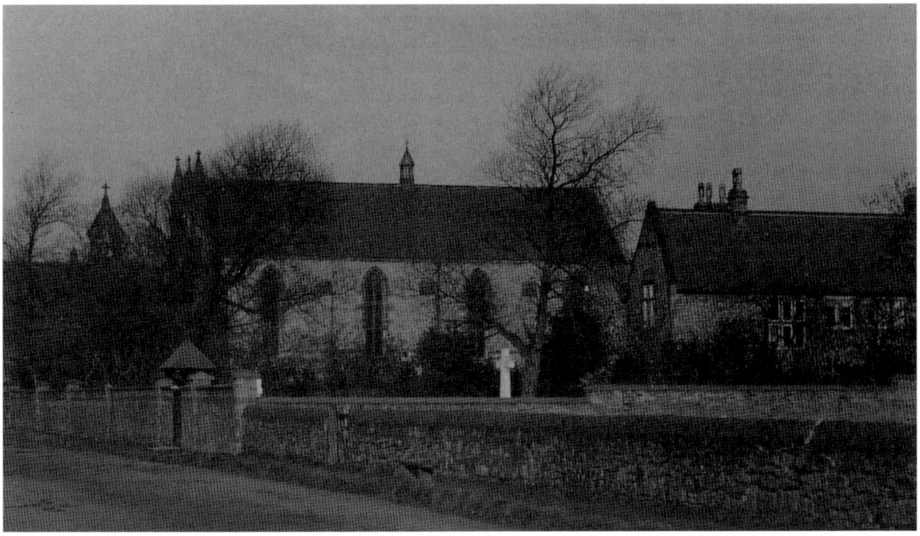

St Michael's Roman Catholic Church on Durham Road, circa 1910. The Church opened on November 7th 1837 having been designed by Ignatius Bonomi, an architect who worked on Lambton Castle and many other well known northeast landmarks, churches and bridges, including Durham Castle and Durham Prison.

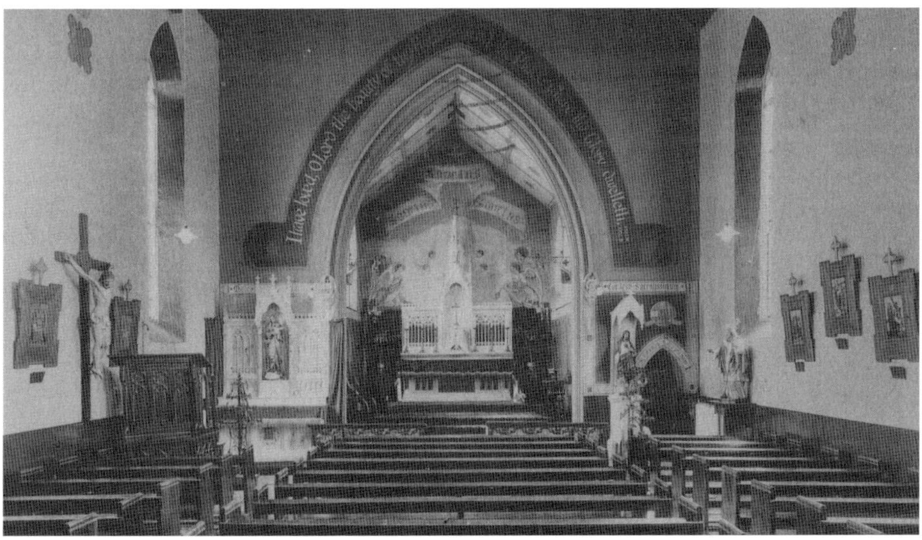

An early view of the interior of St Michael's Roman Catholic Church, circa 1920. Originally the Church occupied the upper floor and it was customary for women to sit on the right and the men on the left. The lower floor was occupied by a school.

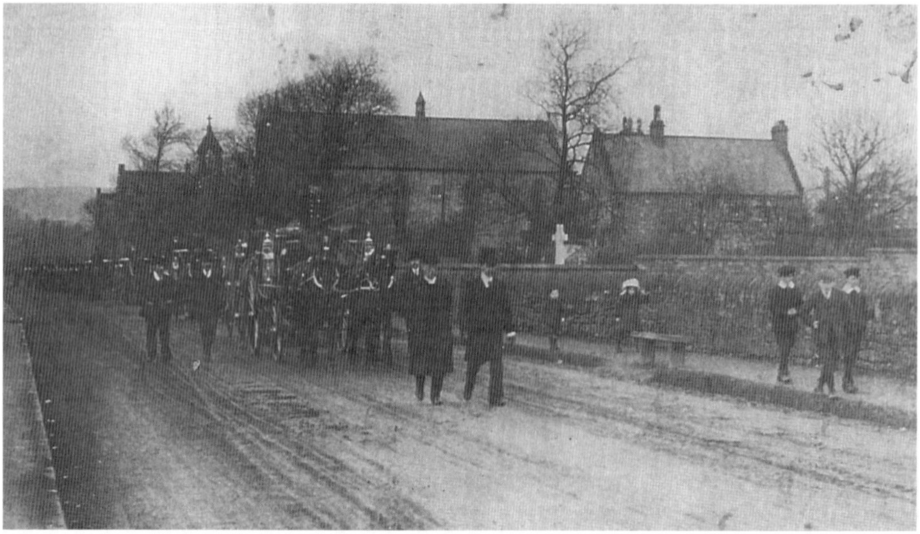

The funeral cortege of the late George Scott of 26 Outram Street passes along Durham Road on its way to the municipal cemetery on February 25th 1912. The Catholic Church and school can be seen in the background.

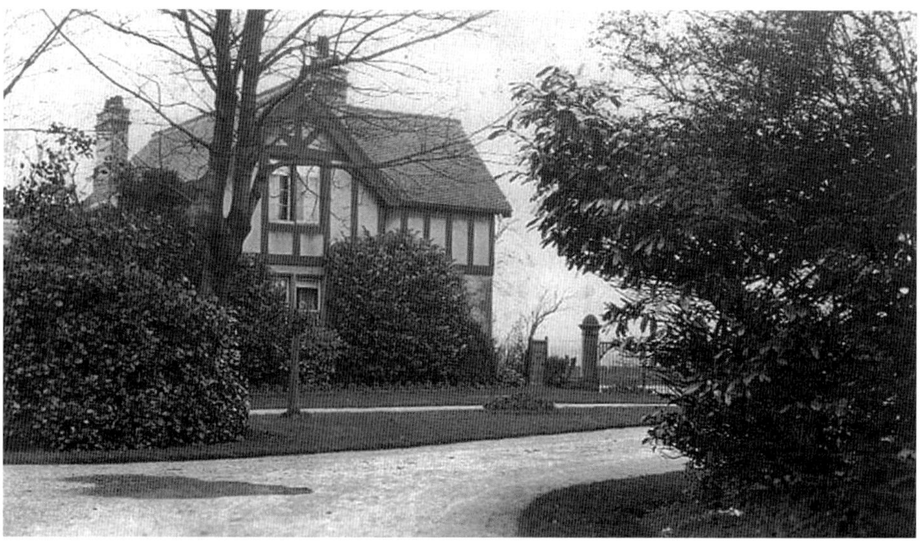

The cemetery keeper's lodge on Durham Road in 1939. The cemetery opened on March 1st 1892 at a cost of £4000. The first burial was for seven month old James Nicholson of Chilton Moor. The new cemetery offered an alternative burial ground to the Church's overcrowded Hillside Cemetery, though it was not consecrated until 1907.

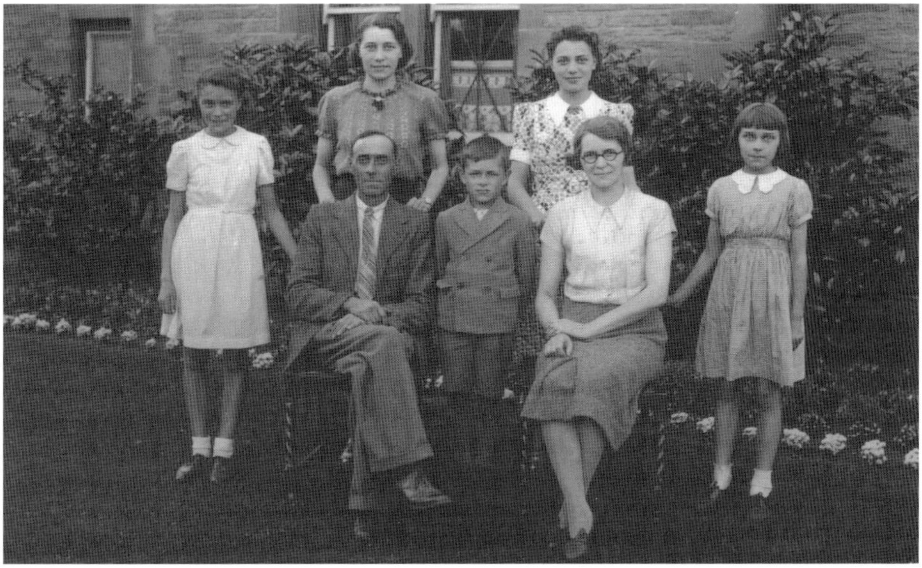

August William Cooper, cemetery superintendent, and his wife Ellen in the grounds of the cemetery lodge, circa 1939. Also pictured are their children, from left to right: Vera, Marion, William, Gladys and Norah.

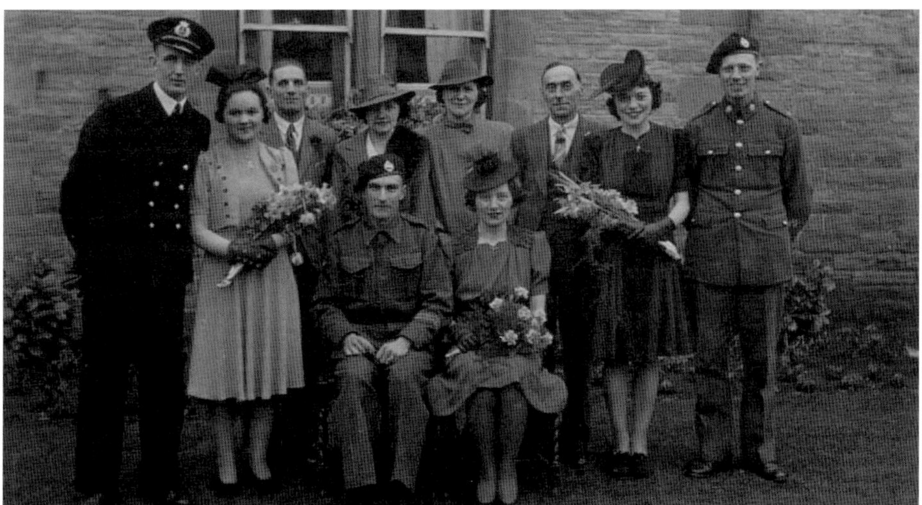

The bride, groom and guests pose for a rare wartime photograph outside the Durham Road cemetery lodge at the wedding of Marion Cooper and Peter Meech on February 14th 1942. Behind the seated groom are his parents, Sidney and Lillian Meech, and behind the seated bride are her parents, Ellen and August Cooper, and her sister, Gladys Cooper with an unidentified man.

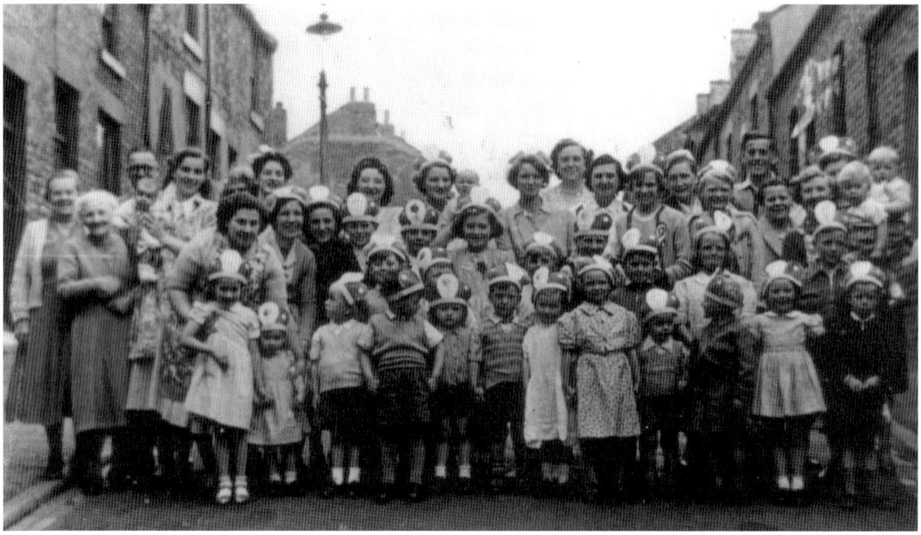

A party on Robinson Street to celebrate the Coronation of Queen Elizabeth II on June 2nd 1953. Seen at the front left are Phyllis Holmes and her two daughters, Helen and Lorna (smaller of the two).

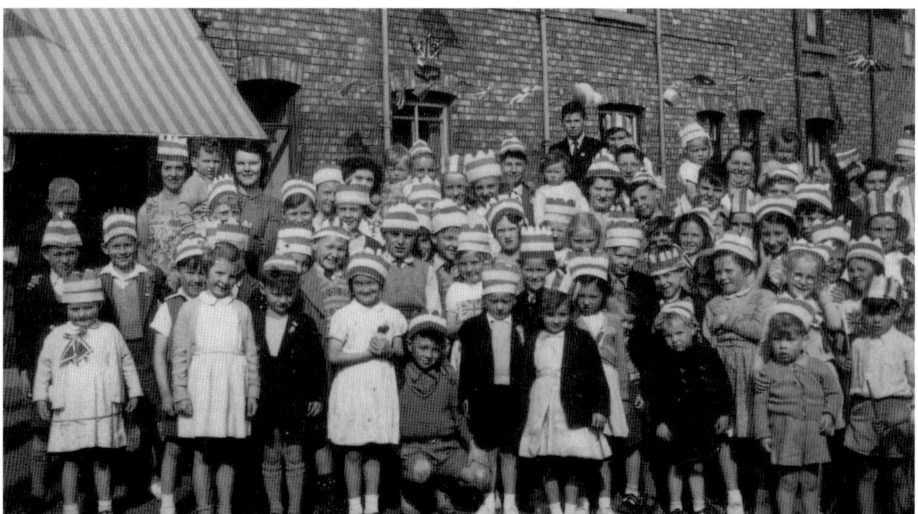

It would seem that all of Houghton was celebrating the Coronation, as this similar photo of Outram Street's party shows. Pictured are: Front Row - Judith Lamb (second girl from left); and Carol Simms (third girl from the left). Back Row - Audrey Brown holding her young son, Cliff (under the awning).

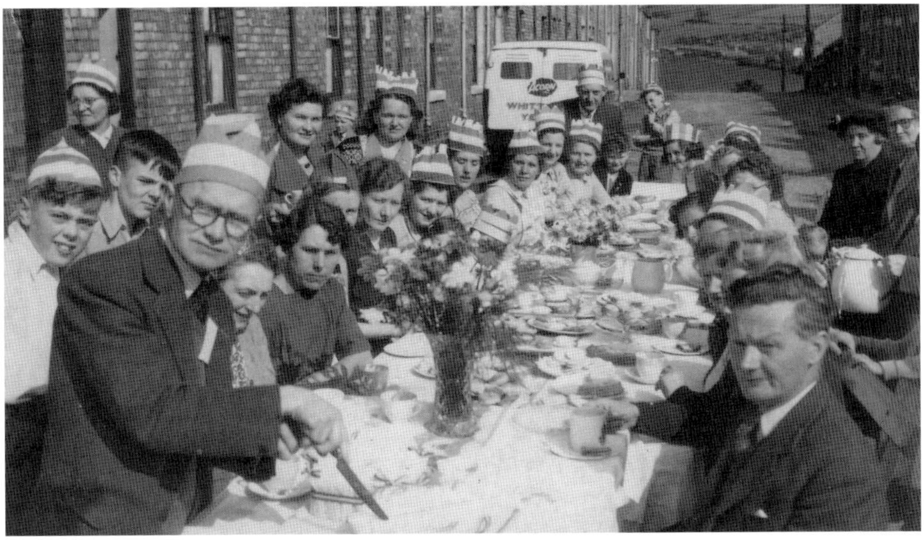

Residents prepare to break bread at the Outram Street Coronation party in 1953. Rev George Smith is cutting the cake while his son stands behind him wearing one of the many homemade party hats. The gentleman sitting at the front right is Billy Crisp who had a bakery on Outram Street (and provided the bread on the table). The two ladies next to the lady with the teapot are the Misses Florrie and Edith Elton.

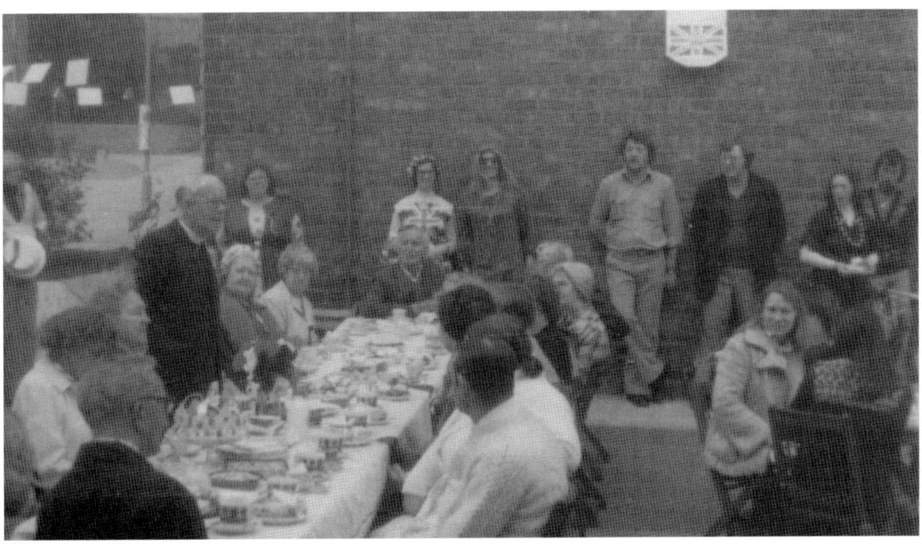

Houghton continues to hold Her Majesty in great affection as this 1977 photo of the Balfour Street Silver Jubilee party shows. The gentleman standing at the table is Rev Vince Woodhill, with his wife Lillian to his left. Can anyone identify the other residents in these photographs?

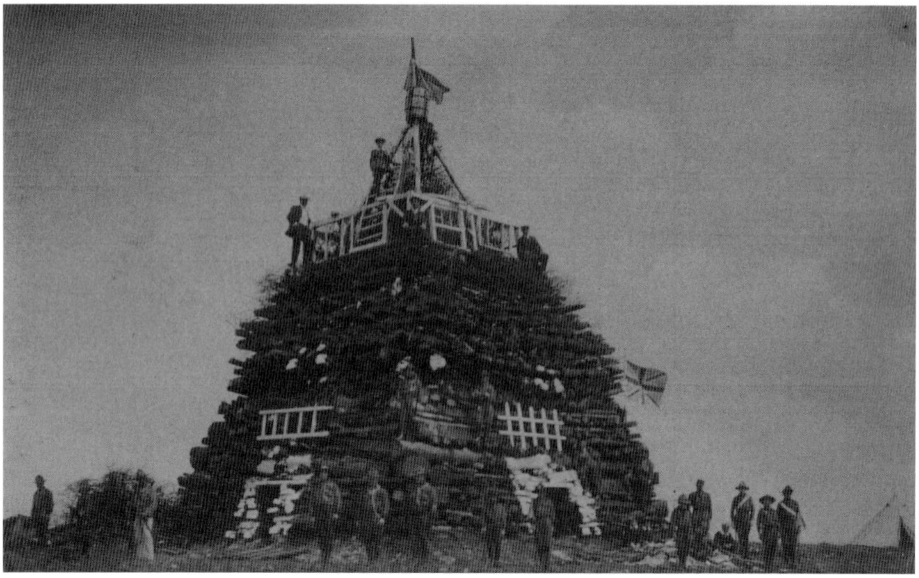

Leslie Holbrook surveys the rooftops of Houghton from the top of the Coronation Bonfire on Houghton Hill, June 22nd 1911. The bonfire measured fifty foot in height, with a base measuring thirty foot by thirty foot, and was made from 150 tons of material. The bonfire was built as part of the local celebrations for the Coronation of George V.

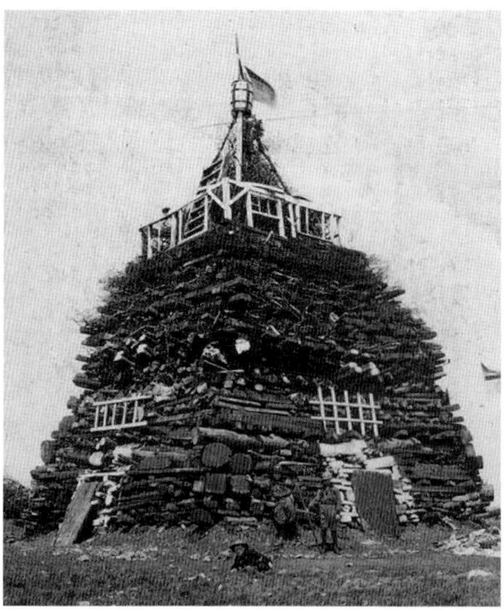

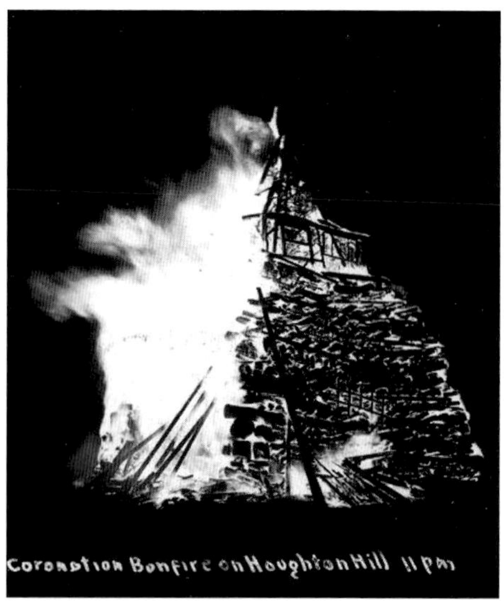

The local Scouts were charged with keeping an eye on the monster before it was set alight at eleven o'clock that night. The flames could be seen for miles.

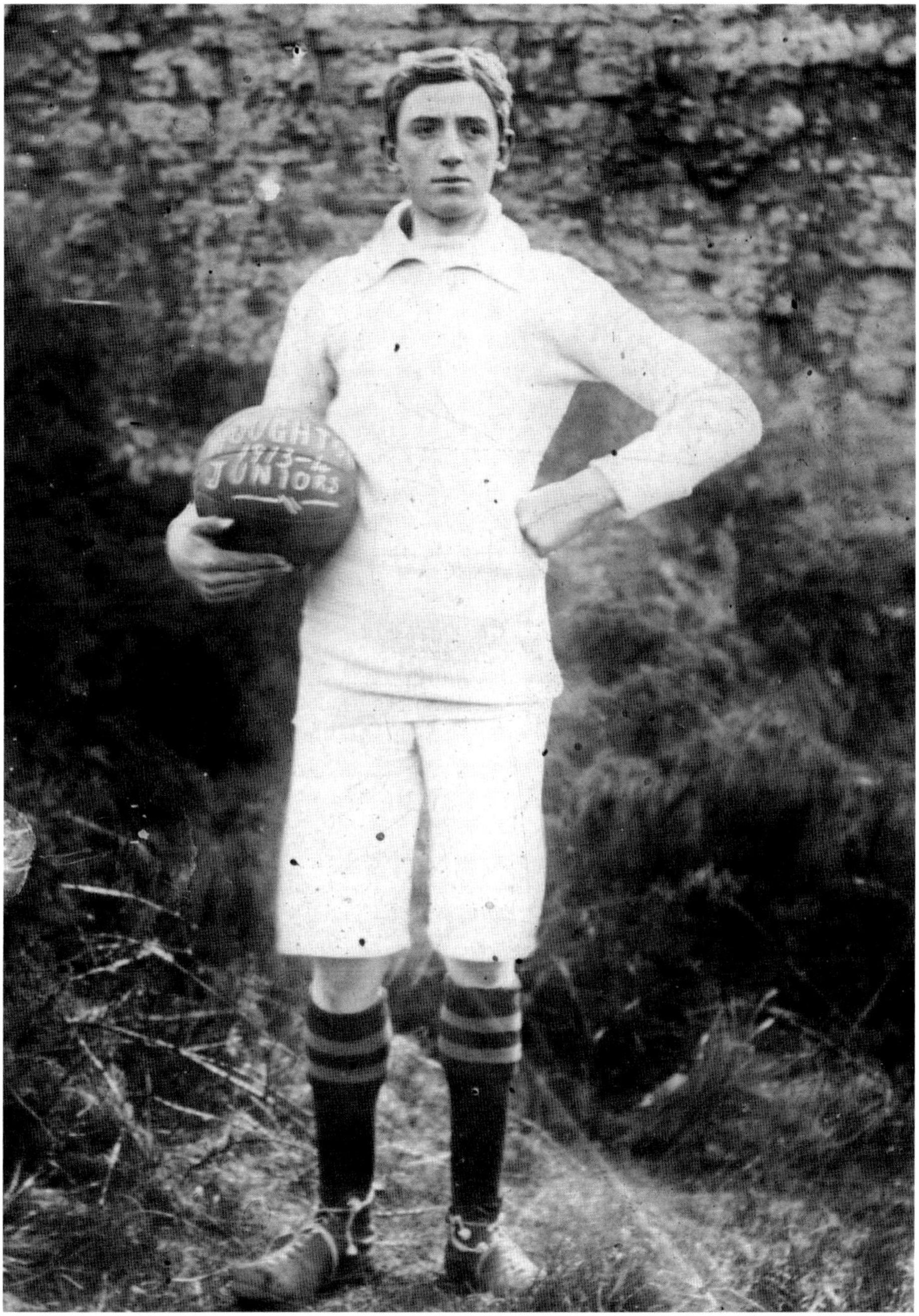

A young lad from Houghton Juniors football team poses during the 1913 - 1914 season. Note the magnesian limestone rocks in the background. Was the photo taken up by the hillside?

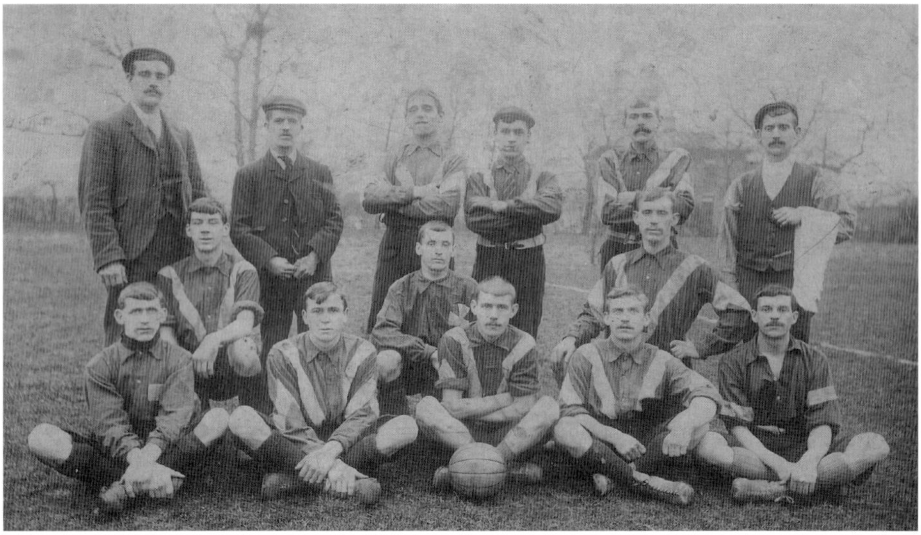

Football was a favourite pastime amongst Houghton's many miners and several teams and leagues existed across the coalfields. This unidentified team in the late 1800s is one such example. Two players have been identified in the front row: C. Scott (second from left) and R. Dawson (second from right).

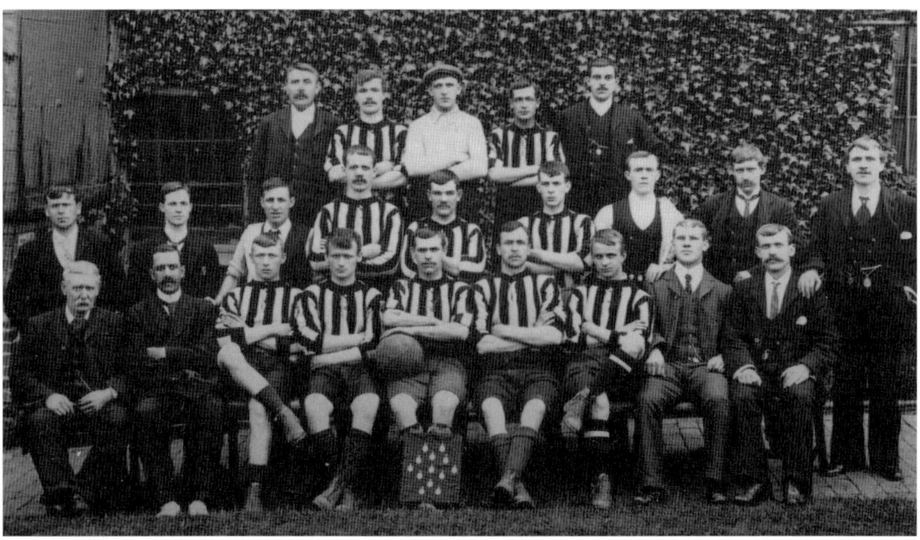

Houghton Rovers Association Football Club during the 1904 - 1905 season. Pictured are, from left to right: Front Row - R. D. Marshall; Dr Langenberg; R. Marshall; W. Brandford; J. Beston; C. Scott; S. Coxon (Sec & Vice Captain); T. Shields (Vice President); and R. Dawson (Treasurer). Middle Row - Fred Scott; R. Roxby; D. Linden (Trainer); W. Wardle; J. Miller; R. Fenton; R. Delap (Trainer); W. Vickers; and J. Lowrif (Chairman). Back Row - T. Atkinson; M. Kimmite; J. Ferris; R. J. Roxby; and R. Stoves.

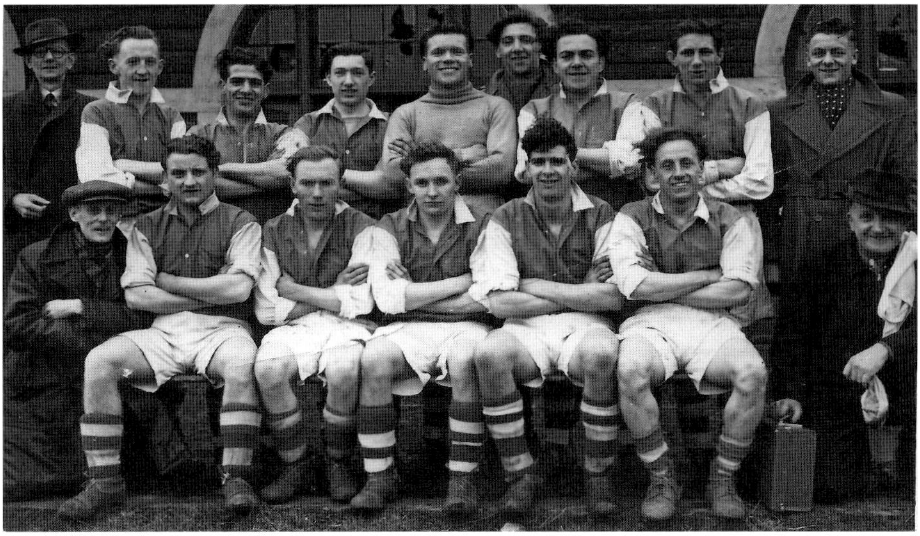

Houghton Wednesday football team outside the Welfare Hall's sports pavilion, 1951. The team was so called because the league took place on a Wednesday afternoon when many businesses and shops in the Houghton district were closed. Some of the players seen here include: Front Row - Jimmy Charlton (second from left) and Alf Ball (third from left). Back Row - Freddie Gordon (third from right) and Billy Gallagher (fifth from right). Frank Forester, who was injured and didn't play, can be seen in the back row wearing the overcoat.

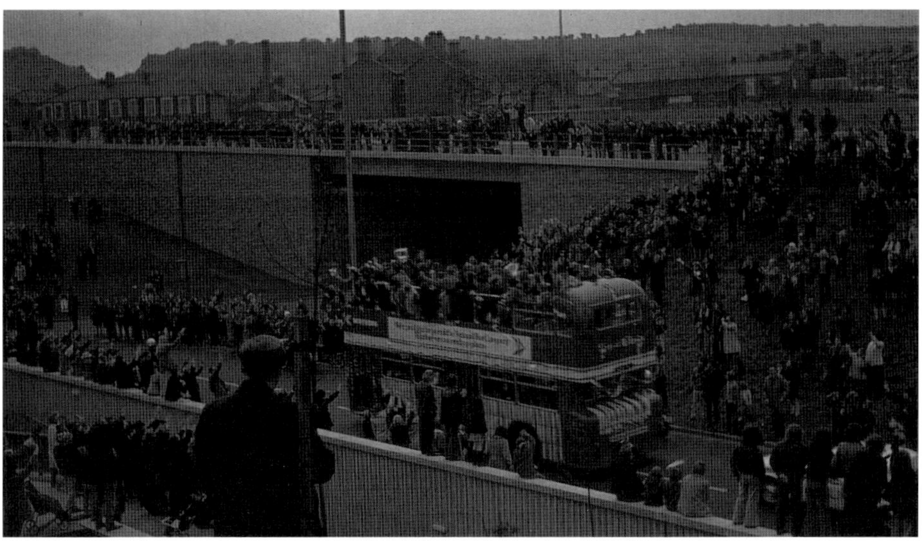

Thousands of people line the bank side of the A690 as Sunderland AFC's victory parade bus passes through Houghton on the team's triumphant return with the FA Cup in May 1973.

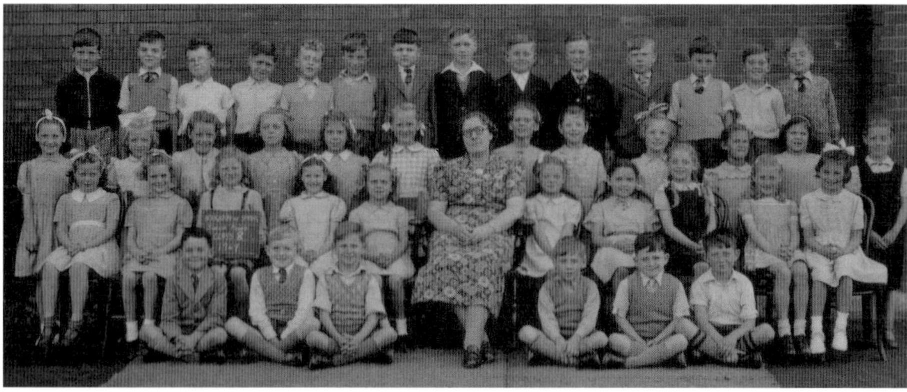

Miss Florrie Hissett and class 8 from Houghton Junior Mixed School, Newbottle Street, 1949. Many of the children in the photograph have been identified and include: Back Row - David Stephenson; Derek Lamb; David Taylor; unknown; William Straughair; Peter Conn; John Brereton; Jonathan Jackson; Keith Tate; Kenneth Daley; unknown; Kenneth Hall; Michael Plews; and Clive Hamilton. Middle Row - Brenda Cole; Pat ?; unknown; unknown; Jean Anderson; Patricia Bartlett; Janet Hall; unknown; Patricia Brown; Olga Gavine; Olive Hirst; and Maureen Robinson. Front Row - Joan Lambton; Marie Tarbett; Margaret Grey; unknown; unknown; Miss Florrie Hissett; unknown; Jean Luke; Brenda Nesbitt; Michelle Reed; and Doreen Tubman. Sitting Boys - Barry Hodgson; Peter Dobbie; Arthur ?; Denis Shrimpling; Alan Jones; and Gilbert Medd.

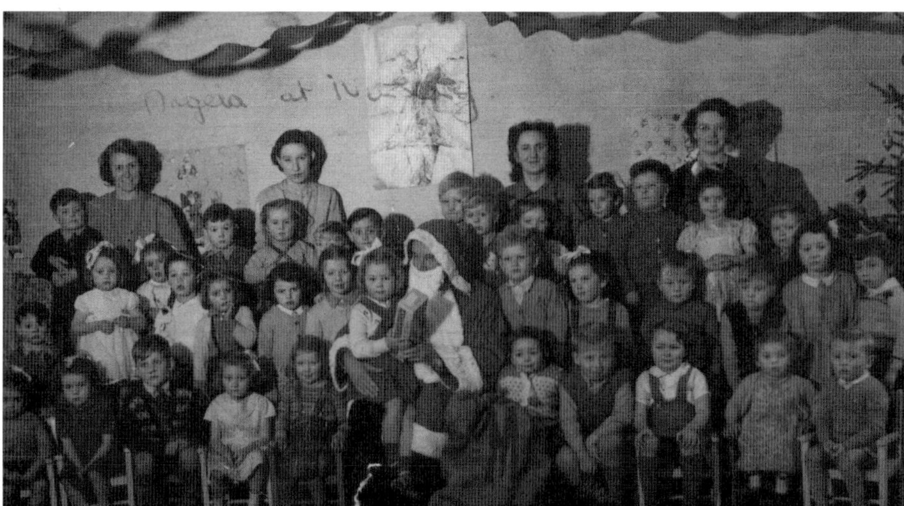

Heather Ramsey sitting on Santa's knee when he made a visit to Houghton-le-Spring Nursery School, Hetton Road, in December 1952. Children identified in the front row include: Angela Muggeridge (second from left); Linda Ramsey (fourth from left); Dorothy Powney (third from the right); and Phillip Michael Doyle (fourth from right). The teacher at the right is Mrs Simpson.

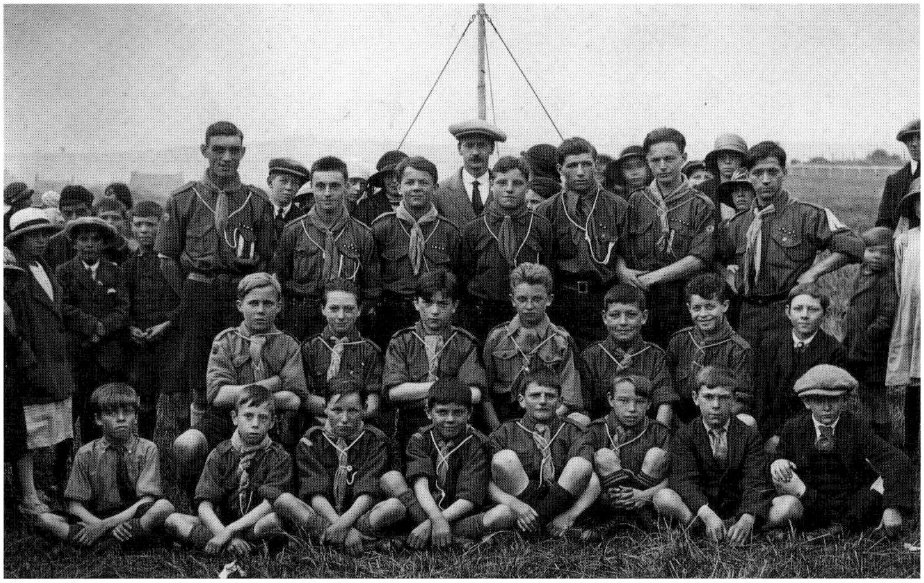

Scouts on Houghton's Racecourse take time out from the carnival to pose for this photo in 1924. The Scouts were helping to raise funds towards the cost of a cenotaph, which was unveiled a year later (see page 15). Many of these faces have been identified and include: Back Row - Andrew Willis; Clive Taylor; Lambton Purvis; Mr William Kidd (Assistant Scout Leader); unknown; unknown; Martin Purvis; and Jack Wanless. Middle Row - George Richardson; Joe Wanless; unknown; Luke Gibson; Jack Pratt; Frank Masters; and Billy Dawson. Front Row - Unknown; Harry Kidd; Billy Leach; unknown; Andrew Devine; Phillip Atwill; Edward Hodgson; and Billy Wilson.

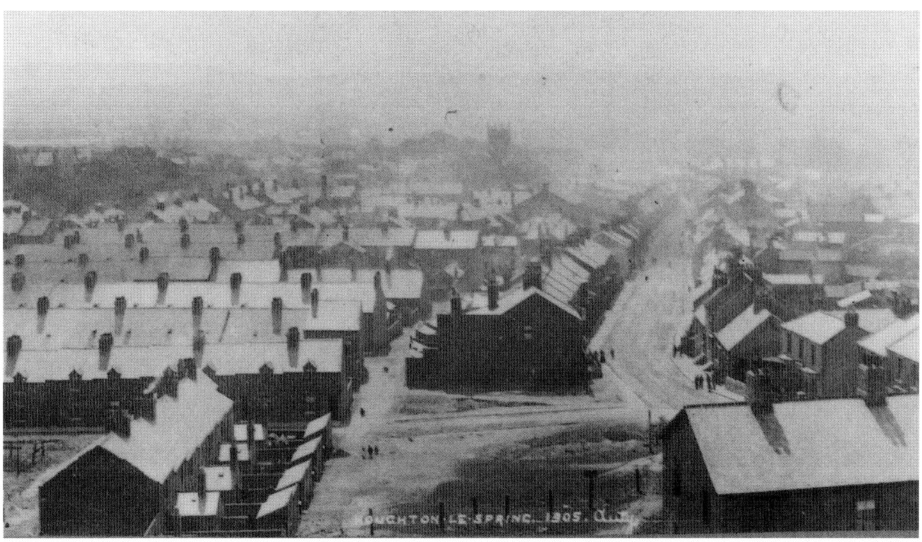

A smoky view of the rooftops of Houghton and many of the now demolished streets, circa 1905.

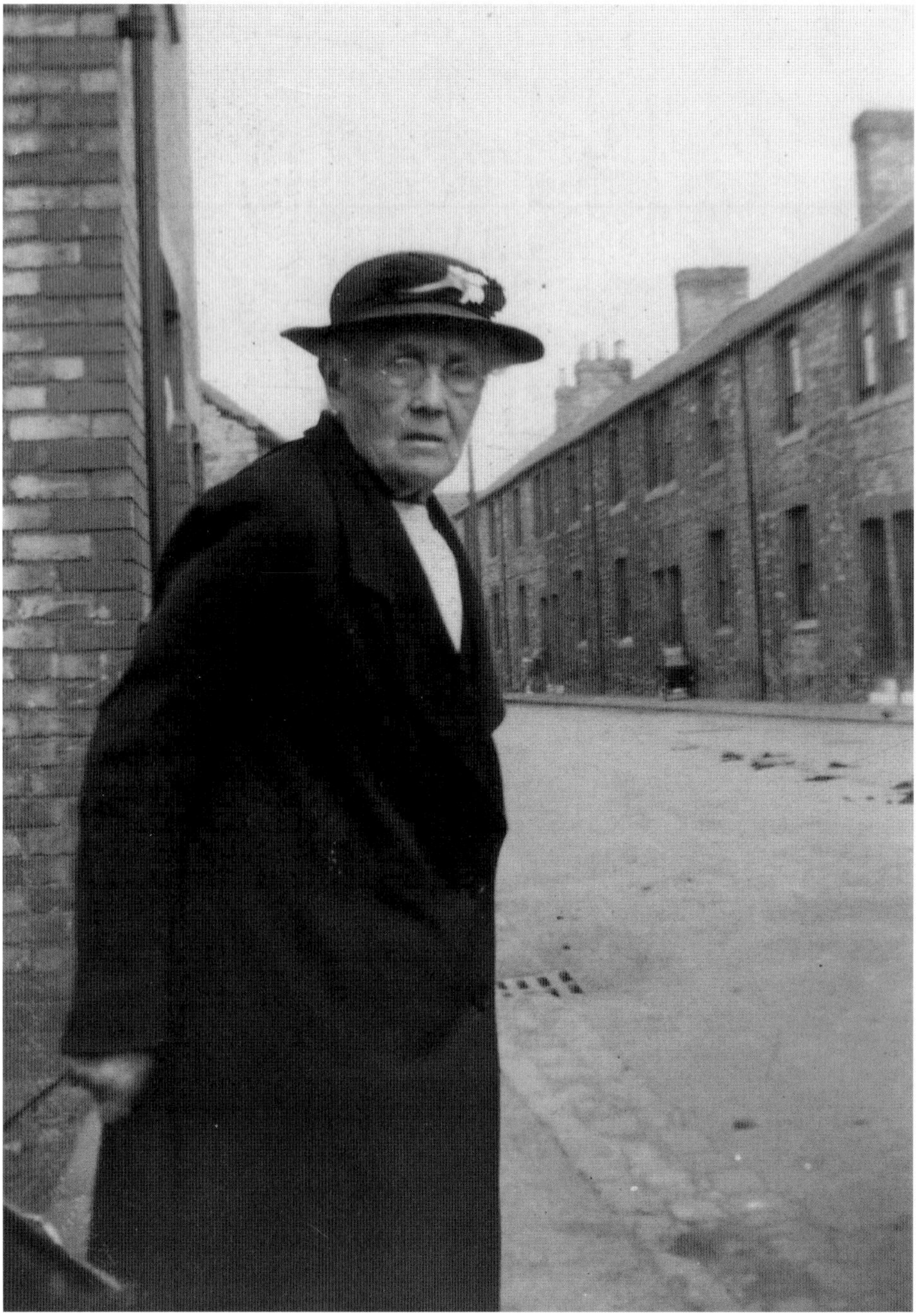

Annie Thompson on Hopper Street in 1938. This street was located where the roundabout now is at the north end of Newbottle Street. It was named after George Hopper, owner of the iron foundry which extended from Sunderland Street. Two public houses could be found on Hopper Street: the Bonnie Pit Lad; and the Prince of Wales, which was known as the Flying Poker.

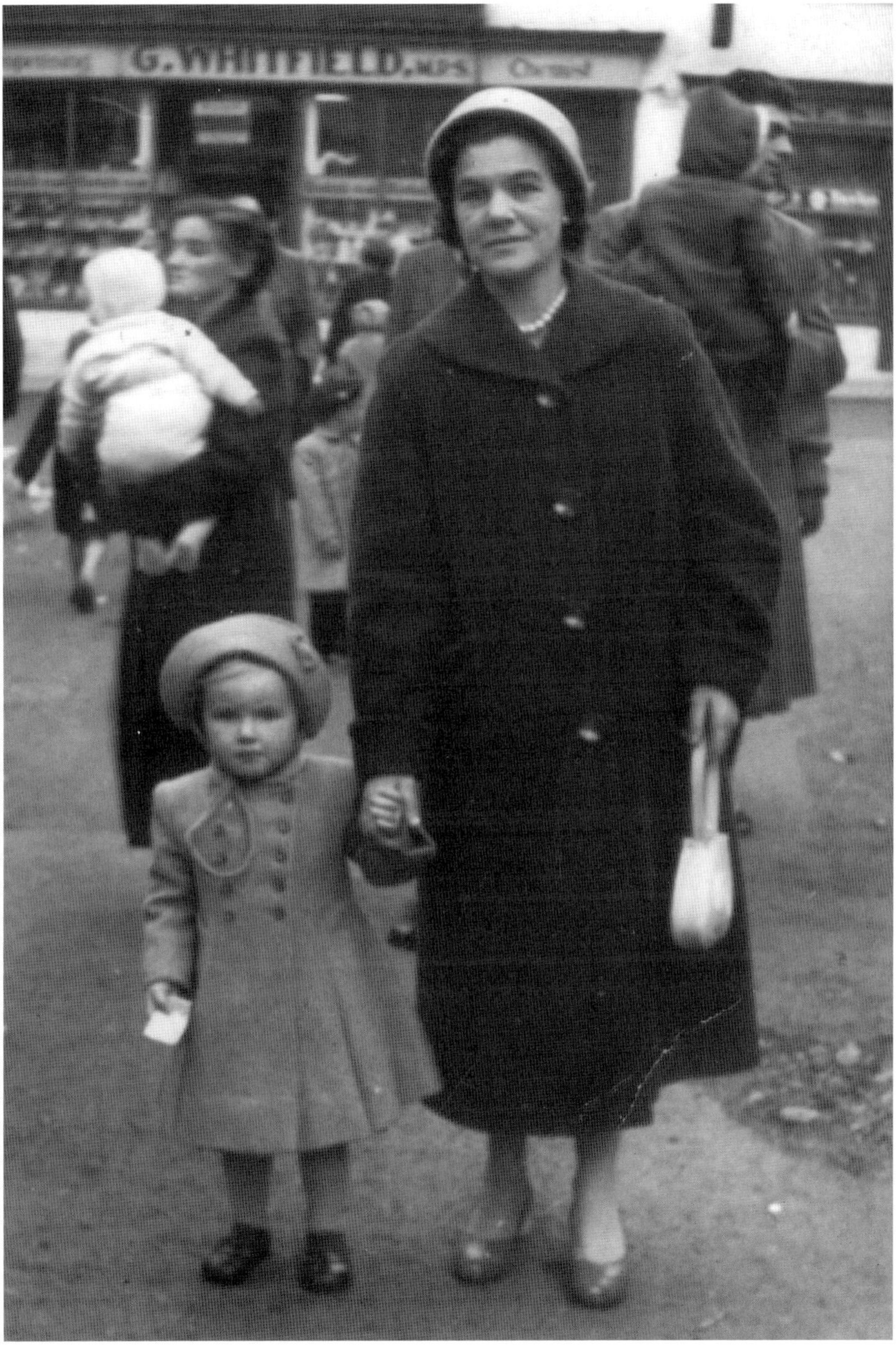

Emily Lanagan and her three year old daughter, Linda, at the entrance to the Lake in October 1958. The shop in the background is G. Whitfield's chemist at the lower end of Sunderland Street.

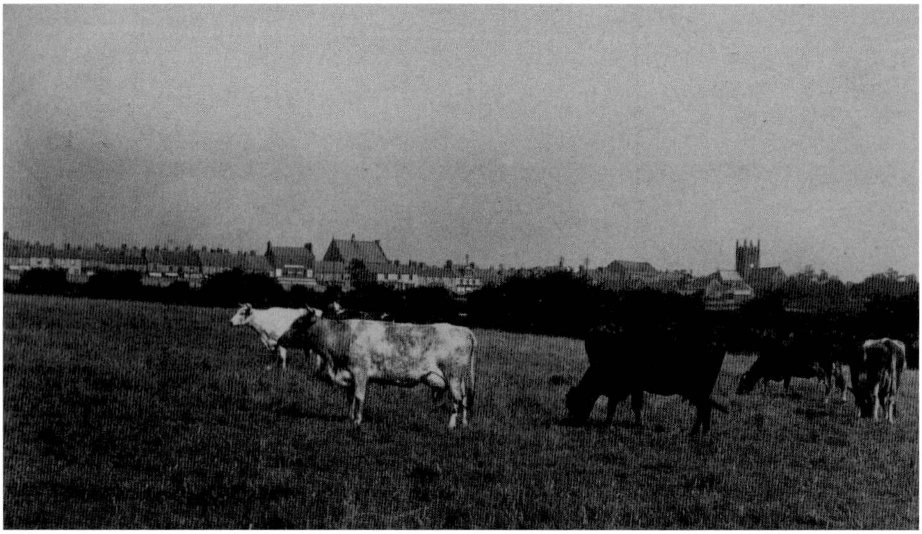

A final glimpse of Newbottle Street in the days before the west side of the street was built. This rare view, from circa 1905, shows cows grazing in a field on land that is now Glebe Terrace on Burn Promenade.

ACKNOWLEDGEMENTS

This book is dedicated to Joan Lambton and Heather Williams, preservers of Houghton's history, and to the memory of Ruth Scott, a Houghton lass who enthusiastically shared her childhood memories of Houghton in the 1940s.

As ever I pay tribute to my forebears, the late Houghton historians Ken Richardson and C. A. Smith. Gentlemen, I salute you and thank you for your legacy and inspiration.

Books like this do not just appear overnight, indeed this selection of photos and captions is only a glimpse at ten years worth of research.

Thanks are extended to all who helped along the way, especially those who kindly loaned their precious photos for copying, but also those who gave memories, advice, support, or even a friendly word in the right direction.

Paul Lanagan would like to place on record his thanks to the following people:
Antonio Angelosanto; Peter Brett; Tom Brett; Linda Bromfield; Stephen Bromfield; Cliff Brown; Mary Buston; Ian Brett Cooper; Lena Cooper; Doreen Crosland; George Davison; Wendy Davison; Emily Forester; Frank Forester; Steven Gee; Michael Grieve; Jan Hanson; Judith Jackson; Adonia Lanagan; Irene Lanagan; Lyndsay Lanagan; Richard Lanagan; Romalli Lanagan; Sabaean Lanagan; Ron Lawson; Alysoun Learmonth; John Robert Learmonth; Melanie Lewis; Lorna Mackenzie; John Mawston; John Price; Sheila Quigley; Peter & Dorothy Riani; Frank H. Rushford; Charles Scott; Kevin Scriven; Douglas Smith; Elizabeth Stevens; Sarah Stoner; Paul Sutherland; Dianne Sutherland; Nicola Thompson; Marion Toy; Alan Vickers; T. Wheatley; Robin Williams; Ron Young; and all the good folk at 1st Houghton (St Michael's) Scout Group.

The author is always on the lookout for photographs and memories. If you would like to contribute to a second volume of this book and are happy to have your photos copied, please contact Paul Lanagan by email on: info@houghtonheritage.co.uk